All-Day Singing
&
DINNER on the GROUND

All-Day Singing & DINNER on the GROUND

Willadeene Parton

Rutledge Hill Press
Nashville, Tennessee

Published in Nashville, Tennessee, by Rutledge Hill Press, Inc., 211 Seventh Avenue North, Nashville, Tennessee 37219. Distributed in Canada by H. B. Fenn & Company, Ltd., 34 Nixon Road, Bolton, Ontario L7E 1W2. Distributed in Australia by Lothian Books, 11 Munro Street, Port Melbourne, VIC 3207. Distributed in New Zealand by Tandem Press, 2 Rugby Road, Birkenhead, Aukland 10. Distributed in the United Kingdom by Verulam Publishing, Ltd., 152a Park Street Lane, Park Street, St. Albans, Hertfordshire AL2 2AU.

Cover and book design by Bateman Design

Typography by D&T/Bailey Typesetting, Inc., Nashville, Tennessee

Library of Congress Cataloging-in-Publication Data

Willadeene.
    All-day singing and dinner on the ground / Willadeene Parton.
        p. cm.
    Includes index.
    ISBN 1-55853-483-0
    1. Parton Family. 2. Willadeene—Family. 3. Cookery—Tennessee. 4. Tennessee—Social life and customs.   I. Title.
    TX649.A1W55 1997
    641.59768—dc21   97-11449
                                                            CIP

Printed in the United States of America

1 2 3 4 5 6 7 8 9 — 02 01 00 99 98 97

Dedication

To my son, Mitchell Blalock, light of my life, and his sweet, beautiful wife, Kathy.

To Papa and my brothers and sisters, David, Denver, Dolly, Bobby, Stella, Cassie, Randy, Freida, Floyd, and Rachel, who have shared with me many of these foods or the lack of them. Also, to my nieces and nephews, aunts and uncles. To the memory of my grandparents.

To my mother, the most creative person I know. She made clothes for us from rags and scraps, which were given to us.

Dolly was the first to tell the story to the public, when she wrote the now famous *Coat of Many Colors.* Mother gave us beauty, joy, and wonder in our youth. We watched a cocoon with fascination, as well as a white, green, or speckled bird egg. Then, when we would see a butterfly or moth, she would make us wonder if maybe we had seen it before it could fly. When we heard the birds sing or watched them fly from tree to tree, we hoped we had seen the eggs or the baby birds before they left the nest.

The kitchen was where she did the best and most magic. She was good! She had heard the story of stone soup sometime in her youth. Well, it became our very own. We would actually find a stone from the small stream of water that we called the branch (or creek). We scrubbed it clean and dropped it into the soup pot first, then added some water and salt. From there it took on a magic only for us. The story started with a stingy old woman and a poor, hungry old man. Of course, his coat was black and didn't fit very well. Some of the buttons were missing and a hole was in the sleeve near the elbow. The sleeves were short, as was the coat, because it had belonged to someone else before him. He was all bent and twisted with a crooked cane. By the time Mother was finished with the description of the old woman and man, we were helping him trick her into putting just one more potato, onion, tomato and whatever else we might have in the kitchen or garden, into the pot. And, of course, we had to help eat it all before the old woman realized she had been tricked.

Stone Soup

Put one clean scrubbed stone into 1 quart of water.
Add:

6	large potatoes, quartered	1	stick of butter (¼ pound)
6	medium onions, chopped		

Cook the mixture until the potatoes are tender.
Add:

1	teaspoon black pepper	1	46-ounce can tomato juice

Mix:

2	teaspoons sugar	2	teaspoons flour
1	teaspoon cornmeal	2	teaspoons salt

Make a thin paste with a little water. Add this paste to the potato mixture and simmer for a few minutes.
Add:

1 small container of heavy cream or 1 small can of evaporated milk

Simmer for a few minutes. Remove stone. Serve hot with corn bread or saltine crackers. Serves 10 to 12.

Contents

Foreword

Well, here I go again. Deene, as I call my *older* sister Willadeene, has written another book about our family, and I'm proud that she asked me to write something about it.

I've just been reading the manuscript, and I'll tell you, it's made me hungry and happy and a little sad. Hungry because all those recipes that I grew up with sound so good. Happy because she tells some more wonderful stories about our family and what it was like growing up in our Tennessee mountains with a passel of Partons. Sad because time is moving on for all of us. But Deene's new book does take me back to good times.

It's fun for me to look back at those times, which seem so long ago in one sense and so close in another. I enjoy remembering what it was like growing up in the South—with all of our Southern "quirks" and "fancies" and our special Southern sense of family. Now that doesn't mean that only Southern folk will enjoy this collection of Parton family recipes and the stories that go along with them. No—Momma Deene has many special gifts, but most particularly she understands and can communicate the nature of our family's individual experience.

I think it's wonderful to find out that no matter how many different kinds of individuals there are in this country—in the South and the West and the North and the East and the Midwest—there's only one kind of people. If we let ourselves be, we're all brothers and sisters, and we can be part of one big family. I think that's a big part of what Deene has done here in sharing our family's stories and recipes and how we grew up. Yes, it is Southern, but it is still just part of a family picture that travels far beyond our Smoky Mountains and embraces those things that are still good about this country.

Once again, thanks, Deene. I love you.

Dolly Parton

Acknowledgments

Special thanks go to Kathy Blalock, Barb McLellan, Dana Smith, Aunt Lillie Owens Huskey, Robin Williams, Bev Ellis, and Dolly.

Special thanks also go to Wayne Ball. He has shared his precious memories of food prepared by his mother, the late Belle Lunsford Ball.

I am grateful to the following friends and family members who have cooked me good meals, shared recipes and photos, and given me encouragement: John Rice Irwin, Patricia McLellan, Cathy McLellan, Mary and Andy Ratkai, Nickie Kinnamon, Stella Parton, Marvin West and his mother, Mrs. Whittaker, Eugene and Charla Honea, Carla Page, Marva Ray, Kristy Ivey, Rachel and Richard Dennison, Deb and Randy Parton, Teri LaFaye, Ann Kirkham, Benita Murphree, Lillian Denton, Aunt Frankie Parton, Aunt Dorothy Jo Owens, Doris Parton, Cassie Seaver, Rose Hurst, Nelle Fine, Roger Harron, Juli Dorland, Sheila Gibson, Debbie Poole, Faye Dunn, Ann Blalock, Donna Lashlee, Dena Bell, Barbara and Shelly Wooliver, Ms. Ledford and daughters Brenda and Linda, Janet Perryman, Julia Crumley, Phyllis Crumley, Tammy Styles, Ellen Long, Bonnie Loan, June Roper, Grace Stallings, Emma Adair, Carolyn Sadler, Dollywood, Myrtle Rhinehart, Hazel Putman, Russert Cullen, Ron Bechman, Judy Kilby, Shelby Lester, Helen Walden, Ruth Murchison, Linda Lewanski, Joan Riggs, Jean Valentine, Mary Lou Underwood, Molly Robinson, B. J. Steltemeier, Dean Buttrey, Ellen Hoover, Martha Ashcraft, Janine Roushey, Martha Reagan, Veda Overton, Myrna Malicoat, Charlie and Betsy Mangrum, Sandi Noble, Marita Beeman, Dennis Carney, and Freida Parton.

I also wish to acknowledge the following people for their help in obtaining period photographs: Roger Harron; Ann Evans Alley, Karina McDaniel, Wayne Moore, and Julia Rather at the Tennessee State Library and Archives; and Sally R. Polhemus at the McClung Historical Collection, Knox County Public Library.

If I have left anyone out, I am truly sorry and will catch you in the next book. Thank you so much.

Introduction

I grew up in east Tennessee. This is a part of the rural South that is much different from the rest of Tennessee, and much different from the rest of the South in many ways. Yet in many ways it is also the same.

Mountain folk and hill folk—yes, there is a difference—in east Tennessee are a fiercely independent lot. Now, generally, southerners are a fiercely independent lot, but their reasons may and do vary quite a bit.

For instance—in west Alabama there were a lot of what people often called poor dirt farmers. Most often, they were poor in the sense of not having much money, but originally the term referred to the quality of the soil they had to farm. In the hills and the mountains of east Tennessee, there were a lot of what people often referred to as "hard-scrabble" farmers. They had to "scrabble hard" for a living—usually because the land off which they had to live might be rocky—hard scrabble—or just worn out. It was surely not the delta-rich land of west Tennessee, even though we do have some dark, rich soil in the foothills where we live. Different ways of having to live and survive make different kinds of folk.

I was not a child of the depression in the sense of having grown up and lived through the "Great Depression." It was my parents who had to do that. But in the hills and mountains of east Tennessee where we lived, the Depression—in one sense—started long before 1929 and lasted long after the rest of the country had "recovered."

Some of the recipes I have collected for this book are more than 100 years old. So, you see, my people have been living hard scrabble lives for a long time. Somehow, though, our mother, and our mother's mother, and her mother, and our father's mother, and her mother, and so on—they knew the foods to fix to keep their children and grandchildren alive and as healthy as possible. And as I look back on these recipes and the events and times they relate to in the life of my family, I recognize that the sustenance they represent was for our souls as well as our bodies.

Now, none of us kids were ever over-fed or over-weight—that's for sure. We depended on the foods we grew or gathered wild from the fields and hills around our home. Our papa hunted and fished to help put meat on the table.

We grew sugar cane for molasses. We kept bees for honey, and we sold what we didn't use ourselves. We learned what flowers and herbs and plants to use for our own medicines. We made tonics from chamomile or licorice or dandelions. We tried to cure colic with catnip tea or ginger tea or sassafras tea. We treated headaches and other pains with valerian, catnip, comfrey, ginger, and chamomile.

Music was always a part of our get-togethers. This picture of Judge Taft and his mountain band was taken in 1938 in Spencer, Tennessee, which is on the Cumberland Plateau near McMinnville. (Courtesy of Tennessee State Library and Archives)

And we used herbs to enhance the natural flavors of the foods we ate. If you aren't familiar with some that are used in these recipes, you may want to use small amounts of them to begin with.

In our family—as in much of the South—food and cooking and family recipes are about more than just eating. Eating—in fact—has always been about more than just eating.

This is because we—as a family—"came together" to eat; and as communities we "came together" to eat. Often, as we worked and went to school and did our chores, the only times we might all be gathered together would be at supper time. And, of course, we weren't eating in front of the TV. We concentrated on each other and the food before us.

And community events were centered around meals: church suppers, all day singing and dinner on the ground, funerals—yes, funerals. Nothing will send a southern cook into the kitchen faster than a death in the family or the neighborhood or the community. There were no funeral homes or such fancy-like places. If your great-grandmother died, she was laid out in the living room—or parlor if you had one—while a feast was laid out in the dining room or kitchen. It was a feast brought by your family and friends and neighbors. "Visitation" was at the home, and people came bearing their best dishes as well as their grief.

I think some of our good people who work with the poor and the homeless understand that you can't save someone's soul if their "belly" is empty. It was an instinctive psychology that we applied in times of stress and grief, as well as in just getting through everyday life.

Food may not have been the "tie that binds" in the communitarian South. But the preparation of food—the caring and love and neighborliness that goes into that preparation—whether it is for a sick friend or a grieving relative or for your family at Christmas or for your child to take to school for lunch—is one of the most important ties that bound us together as a family and as a community. Whether it is secular or religious, the meals that we share as families or neighbors or communities are sacramental. Fourth of July picnics, Labor Day barbecues, community fish fries, Thanksgiving dinner, Christmas dinner—all of these are more than just "meals" to satisfy our physical hunger. Our best instincts as human beings are for sharing what we have and what we are with our family and our friends and our neighbors.

That is what these recipes represent for me. They are the history of my family, about how we lived and shared and loved each other. And I want to share them with you—whether you use them and prepare these dishes for your family and friends or whether you just enjoy reading and collecting recipes. Recipes like these that are passed on from generation to generation really are about more than

Enjoying watermelon on the porch in Morgan County, Tennessee. (Courtesy of Tennessee State Library and Archives)

"only" eating. They are a social and family history, and I think it's important to preserve these things.

So, that is one reason that I have not "tinkered" too much with some of the recipes. Some of the ingredients in the recipes may seem "quaint," but I have tried to preserve the sense of time these may communicate. Others may not be as specific with the steps or instructions, but again I believe it is important to leave these as they were handed down as much as possible. Cooking can—and often should be—instinctive. That is reflected sometimes in the paucity of detailed instructions. Really, I'm not being just lazy.

Finally, I just hope this book will be a friendly trip for you through some Parton family history. I'm proud of my family, and so I'm proud to share my family with you through these recipes and stories. Enjoy and come back for seconds.

I hope you will feel free to substitute light oils and salt seasoning as well as less sugar in some of these recipes. The foods are even more tasty to most everyone now with these adjustments. Many of these recipes represent how our people had

to cook in the past. I want to preserve and share these ways of cooking and these recipes. So that's how I put them in the book.

The recipes in this book don't call for a lot of different types of ingredients. For one thing, we didn't have a lot of ingredients or utensils, so you won't need a lot of either to prepare these recipes.

My parents did well in feeding their large family, but words like pâté, croquette, beef Wellington, flan, crêpes, polenta, or liverwurst don't appear here. We enjoyed some very similar foods but we simply called them by other names like liver mush, liver loaf, headcheese, souse, roast pork, mush, custard, pork patties, jellyrolls or fritters.

Of course, we never had all the many foods in this book while we were growing up, but the dishes my mother cooked for us out of necessity tasted wonderful to us. I don't know how she fixed them, but they tasted marvelous to a bunch of hungry children. When asked about some special food she fixed then, she just says, "I don't remember. I just cooked, prayed, and put a handful of love in it." So, a lot of the foods we had and loved can never be recreated by anyone else. But we remember them. And Mother will still prepare them for us sometimes.

We often say, if a person had to be stranded in some desolate place, our parents would have been the people to be there with.

All-Day Singing
&
DINNER on the GROUND

All-Day Singing and Dinner on the Ground

It seems that many of our southern/mountain gatherings and traditions combine equal parts of eating and religion. An all-day singing with dinner on the ground has a lot in common with Decoration Day and with visitations when someone has died. There's food—a lot of it—and a gathering of friends and neighbors and family and a lot of "heavenly" celebrating.

An all-day singing varies some from community to community. In some places, it is very much a one-day "revival" or what we used to call a "camp meeting." Sometimes, it may be the culmination of a week-long revival. Sometimes an all-day singing is just that—it lasts all day and is all singing interrupted only for dinner. In some places, an all-day singing includes some preaching and what is called "personal testimony." But wherever it takes place and no matter the local form it takes, there is always food, food, food. And in my memory, it was always good, good, good.

In some areas, including our mountains, we had—and still have—what is called "harp" or "note" singing. The folks sing to the sounds of the notes—not the words. Grandpa Jake Owens was a music teacher, and he went to a lot of these singings, and we sometimes went along with him. Now we didn't always go just for the singing—we went for the dinner too. Mother would pack two separate picnics. The kids always had a separate bag or shoe box with our very own picnic. Later some of the same dishes would be laid out on a sheet or quilt on the ground or on a table in the churchyard. I remember a lot of fried chicken and biscuits and deviled eggs or pickled eggs. There were green beans with new potatoes, okra, corn,

corn bread, and sometimes corn bread with slices of fried fatback. There were cucumbers and tomatoes—these singings were almost always in the summer.

At our house when there was a revival, dinner usually "extended" into supper because we had gone to church at 10:00 in the morning and then again in the evening. I can remember walking to or from church in the dark carrying flashlights and lanterns. My grandparents told us about "brush arbors" and meetings when people carried a pine torch for light and about how resin smelled when it mixed with the smoke on a warm night. Sometimes, they built a large fire for light for the preacher to preach by.

In this country, religion, in whatever form and whichever region, has always been a part of everyday life. In the South, it seems it was a bigger part—particularly in the rural South. And the practice of religion in the South was almost invariably connected with good food—and plenty of it—and family—and usually plenty of it—and celebrating all three things—religion, food, and family—in a very special way. It's very much a part of my memories of our family and our growing up. I'm glad to share it with you.

- What's a smidgen? It's a very, very small amount.
- How many glasses of punch does this make? Just put it in a big jar and use.
- This dough is too thick to suit me or this batter is too thin. Just add or subtract liquids.
- A generous dash of anything doesn't mean a little or a lot. It means as much as you want. The same thing with a dash or pinch of salt, pepper, or whatever—it's geared to your liking.
- A small amount of butter can be almost anything from 1 teaspoon to ½ cup.
- A scant measure is just "almost full."
- Sweeping the top of rolls or biscuits with milk or butter means brushing the top with these ingredients.

- If a recipe calls for a #8 size skillet for a pan of bread or casserole and you don't have one, the next size up or down is fine. I promise you it will work.
- If you see something is cooking too fast or too slow with the recipe directions, turn it up or down, for goodness sake!
- If you have fancy vinegars and fresh herbs, add them to your recipes if you like to experiment, and make a recipe of your own for your family. Always garnish with what you like. It just makes a prettier dish.
- If the recipe is to be mixed with broth in which meat or vegetables were cooked, use the amount needed for the consistency desired. (If it needs more or less, then fix it!)

MAIN DISHES

Sweet and Sour Chicken

1 whole chicken cut into pieces	1 tablespoon cornstarch
½ cup sugar	½ teaspoon ginger
Salt	¼ cup soy sauce
Pepper	¾ cup water
⅓ cup lemon juice	

Boil chicken pieces first. Make sauce by mixing remaining ingredients in a large skillet and simmering a few minutes, until thick. Add meat. Cook another 45 minutes. Turn once so they won't stick.

Chicken and Dumplings

1 stewing hen	1 heaping tablespoon shortening
3 cups flour	1 teaspoon salt
1 egg	½ cup cold water

Cut chicken for stewing. Barely cover with water and cook until tender for about 2 hours. Remove chicken from stock and remove bones.

Put flour in mixing bowl. In center of flour put egg, shortening, and salt. Gradually add cold water. Work plenty of flour into dough. Roll thin and cut in 2x3-inch strips.

When dumplings are added to stock, lower heat and simmer about 12 to 15 minutes. Place chicken back in the stock. A little butter may be added if chicken is lacking in fat.

Chicken Casserole

2	medium-size chicken breasts, cooked, pulled off bone, and chopped	2	rolls, crumbled
2	celery stalks, diced	1	box Stove Top stuffing Gruel (broth) off chicken
1	large onion, diced	⅔	stick margarine
1	cup corn bread	1	teaspoon sage

Sauté celery and onion in margarine. Put all ingredients in casserole dish and bake in 350° oven for about 30 minutes.

Dolly, Stella, and I always talk about Papa's left-handed gravy. Our Papa is left-handed and when our Mother would be in bed with a new baby, Papa would do the cooking. That was all right for a day or two. He would tell us he made left-handed gravy and biscuits, and that his cooking would make us left-handed like him or pretty or smart. But we missed Mother's cooking, even though Papa does make good gravy. Here is one of his left-handed gravy recipes.

Southern Fried Chicken with Gravy

1	young chicken (3 pounds) Little salt, pepper, lemon juice	2	tablespoons heavy cream Flour Butter or lard
2	eggs		

Clean, dress chicken. Cut in pieces, put lemon juice, salt, pepper over each piece. Dip chicken into beaten egg and cream mixture, roll in flour, fry in butter or lard. Brown chicken, cover pan, cook over slow heat until tender.

Gravy:
Remove chicken; to hot fat add 3 tablespoons flour and 1½ cups thin cream. Season with salt and pepper.

Dolly with my late Aunt Estelle, my mother's sister.

Parmesan Chicken

½ cup fine breadcrumbs
½ cup grated Parmesan cheese
½ teaspoon oregano leaves, crushed
Generous dash garlic powder
Generous dash pepper

4 pounds chicken pieces
2 10¾-ounce cans cream of chicken
or mushroom soup
1 cup milk
Paprika

Combine crumbs, ¼ cup Parmesan, oregano, garlic powder, and pepper. Roll chicken in mixture. Arrange skin-side down in shallow baking pan (15½x10½x2½ inches) or divide between two 2-quart shallow baking dishes (12x8x2 inches). Bake at 350° for 20 minutes. Turn chicken, bake 20 minutes more. Meanwhile blend soup and milk, pour over chicken. Sprinkle with paprika and remaining Parmesan. Bake 20 minutes more or until done. Makes 8 servings.

Southern Fried Catfish

3 large eggs
   Salt to taste
1 teaspoon black pepper
   Dash of cayenne pepper
½ cup milk

2 cups flour
2 cups croutons, crushed, or 2 cups
   cornmeal
24 pieces dressed catfish

Mix eggs, salt, black pepper, cayenne pepper, and milk. Then combine flour and croutons. Dip fish in egg mixture and then in flour mixture. Deep fat fry for 5 minutes at 350° until golden. Place on paper towels to drain. Serve with hush puppies, cole slaw, and corn on cob. Serves 7 to 12.

This was how you had a proper picnic in the 1880s in Knoxville. (Courtesy of Knox County Two Centuries Photograph Project, McClung Historical Collection, Knox County Public Library System)

Cream of Tomato Soup

2 quarts canned tomatoes	1 pint heavy cream
2 cups soup stock	1 pint milk
¼ teaspoon baking soda	Salt
2 teaspoons flour	Celery salt
2 tablespoons butter	Pepper

Put tomatoes and soup stock in kettle, add no water, boil 10 minutes. Strain through colander, add soda, strain through fine colander. Blend flour and butter. In double boiler, heat cream and milk. Combine mixtures and heat. Add water if necessary. Season.

We got dried beans and rice in 2- and 10-pound bags. Macaroni also came in large blue and white boxes. We always had some kind of soup or stew on the stove and a biscuit or piece of corn bread. I bet our young bodies had enough iron to build a bridge. I do know we never ran out of energy or mischief to get into.

Old-fashioned Vegetable Soup

8 large ripe tomatoes	2 tablespoons bacon grease or butter
½ cup chopped cabbage	
1 large potato, diced	1 quart water
½ cup fresh corn	½ cup macaroni (optional)
1 small onion, cut coarse	

Scald tomatoes in hot water to remove peelings. Rinse in cool water. Add tomatoes and other ingredients except macaroni. Let come to a boil, simmer for about 1 hour. Add macaroni after about 40 minutes.

Macaroni and Cheese with Tomatoes

2 cups elbow macaroni	1 teaspoon salt
2 tablespoons butter	½ pound cheese, cubed
2 tablespoons flour	2 large tomatoes
1½ cups milk	Crushed cereal crumbs

Cook macaroni as directed on package. Drain and arrange in an ovenproof Dutch oven, which has been oiled. Using 2- or 3-quart saucepan, make white sauce by melting butter and blending flour; add milk and salt, and bring to boil. Press cheese cubes into macaroni for uniform distribution and arrange tomato wedges over all. Now pour white sauce over slowly, allowing it to run down through mixture. Top with cereal crumbs and bake in moderate oven (350°) for 30 minutes. Serves 6.

Variations:

Tomatoes may be omitted if desired.

Use flaked leftover fish in the recipe for a more complete meal, and for variety.

Omit tomato and add cubes of cooked lobster to convert the recipe into a "guest occasion" dish.

Cabbage Rolls

1 pound ground beef	Pepper
1 pound ground pork	1 large cabbage, leaves separated
1 onion, chopped fine	1 10¾-ounce can condensed tomato soup
1 cup Minute Rice	½ cup water
1 teaspoon dry mustard	
Salt	

Mix first 7 ingredients. Soak cabbage in boiling water to soften leaves. Roll the meat mixture into softened cabbage leaves, roll whatever size you desire. Place in casserole or small roaster. Cover with 1 can condensed tomato soup and water. Bake at 350° for approximately 1½ to 2 hours.

Gladys Parton Boling (left) *and Edith Parton Boling* (right), *both cousins on my father's side of the family, prepare the food for a family reunion.*

Corn Casserole

2   15-ounce cans corn, drained
¼   pound cheese, grated
     Butter, salt, pepper

1   large cup of cracker crumbs
1   cup milk

Put layer of corn in bottom of baking dish. Then add a generous sprinkle of grated cheese, dot with butter, season with pepper and salt. Add a layer of cracker crumbs. Repeat layers over again and then pour milk over. Bake at 350° for about 40 minutes. This is also wonderful made with fresh corn.

Lima Bean Casserole

1½   cups dried lima beans
1   teaspoon salt
1   pound pork sausage, browned or
     fried until crisp
¼   cup molasses

½   cup condensed cream of tomato
     soup
½   cup tomato ketchup
1   teaspoon dry mustard
¼   cup hot water

Wash beans. Cover with cold water. Add salt. Cover, cook slowly until tender. Drain, pour into well-oiled baking dish. Combine remaining ingredients. Add to beans. Bake at 350° for about 1 hour.

Rice and Broccoli Casserole

½ cup onion, chopped
½ cup celery, chopped
4 tablespoons butter or margarine
1⅓ cups chopped broccoli (frozen)

1 10¾-ounce can cream of mushroom soup
1⅓ cups Minute Rice
1 cup Cheeze Whiz

Preheat oven to 350°.

Sauté onion and celery in butter. Butter casserole dish. Parboil broccoli; drain liquid into measuring cup, add water to make ½ cup liquid. Mix soup with all ingredients, pour into casserole dish. Bake at 350° for 30 to 40 minutes. Serves 4 to 6.

Beef Stew Casserole

1 pound stewing beef, cubed
2 cups potatoes, diced
1 cup onions, chopped
1 cup celery, chopped
1 cup carrots, chopped

½ teaspoon salt
2 tablespoons tapioca
1 teaspoon sugar
1 cup vegetable juice or beef bouillon

Mix all ingredients in a casserole dish with a cover. Place in 250° oven for 4 hours. Do not lift lid while cooking.

Ground Beef Casserole

1 pound ground chuck
Small amount of butter
2 cups onions, chopped
2 cups celery, chopped
1 10¾-ounce can cream of mushroom soup

1 10¾-ounce can cream of celery soup
About 2 cups fine noodles

Brown ground chuck in small amount of butter. Sauté onions and celery. Combine onions, chuck, and celery in casserole dish and add mushroom and celery soup. Cook noodles and add to meat mixture. Bake at 350° for 1 hour. Uncover the last few minutes to brown.

Brown Rice Casserole

1½ cups water
⅔ cup brown rice
½ pound bulk pork sausage
1 medium onion, chopped
2 medium peppers, red or green, chopped
½ cup celery, chopped

1 10¾ ounce can cream of mushroom soup
½ cup sour cream
1 cup grated cheese
½ cup minced fresh parsley
½ cup chopped pecans

Bring water to a boil. Stir in rice. Cover and simmer 30 to 40 minutes or until rice is tender and water is absorbed. Crumble sausage in large skillet. Add onion, red or green pepper, and celery. Cook, stirring often, until sausage is browned. Drain. Combine rice, sausage mixture, soup (undiluted), and rest of ingredients. Spoon into greased 11x7x1½-inch baking dish. Bake at 325° for 30 minutes. Serves 6 to 8 people.

My mother, Avie Lee Parton, enjoys the food we have at one of our many family reunions.

VEGETABLES AND SIDE DISHES

Red Rice Casserole

. . . .

4 tablespoons rice	5 slices bacon
1 8-ounce can tomatoes	½ teaspoon salt
4 small onions, sliced	½ teaspoon pepper

Place rice and tomatoes in saucepan, add sliced onions and bacon cut into small pieces. Add 1½ cups hot water. After mixture begins to cook, season and allow to steam for 1½ hours.

Deviled Eggs

. . . .

6 boiled eggs	¼ cup pickle (chopped fine)
2 tablespoons mayonnaise	Paprika
Salt and pepper to taste	6 stuffed olives (optional)
½ teaspoon mustard	

Cut eggs in half lengthwise. Remove yolks to a bowl and mash and blend with remaining ingredients except paprika and olives. Fill each egg half with mixture. Sprinkle with paprika and place half an olive on each half. Makes 12.

Take-Along Potato Salad

. . . .

¾ teaspoon salt	¼ cup mayonnaise
2 tablespoons butter or margarine	⅛ teaspoon black pepper
1 cup boiling water	1 tablespoon chopped green pepper
2 tablespoons cider vinegar	2 tablespoons chopped onion
1 package potato flakes	2 tablespoons chopped celery
¼ cup milk	

Put salt, butter, boiling water, and vinegar in a bowl and add potato flakes. Stir with a fork until completely blended. Add remaining ingredients and stir to mix. If desired, top may be sprinkled with paprika and decorated with slices of hard-cooked egg. Makes 6 servings.

Vegetable Pudding

1 pound bacon
1 large onion
6 large potatoes, peeled and sliced

1 tablespoon flour
2 15-ounce cans corn
1 quart milk

Cut bacon into small pieces and brown. Cut the onion fine and brown in part of the bacon fat. Put in a layer of potatoes, a little flour, a layer of corn, bacon, and browned onion. Repeat until all ingredients are used. Cover with milk and bake at 350° for 45 minutes.

Fresh Lima Beans

6 slices of bacon or fatback, fried until brown
2 cups water
1 onion, chopped

2 cloves garlic, sliced thin
1 green bell pepper, chopped
3 pounds fresh lima beans

Pour most of the fat from the pan in which meat was cooked. Add all ingredients except beans and bacon. Bring to a boil, then reduce heat to simmer. Add lima beans, and cook about 30 minutes or until water has cooked down. Add bacon and serve.

Fried Corn

The creamy consistency of this recipe results from the old "country" method of removing corn from the cob. It is a lot of trouble, but worth every bit of work. Using a very sharp knife, split each row of kernels in half lengthwise, then cut the tops off the kernels. (Be sure to do this over a bowl to catch all the corn and juice.) Holding the cob over the bowl scrape the remaining corn and juice from the cob using the dull edge of the knife blade.

4   tablespoons (½ stick) butter or margarine
2   tablespoons flour

1   teaspoon salt
2   cups fresh corn, prepared as above

Melt butter in a large heavy skillet. Add flour and salt and cook for a few minutes until bubbly. Add corn and stir over low heat until thickened. Cook for 5 to 10 minutes. Serves 4 to 6 people.

Fried Okra

Tumble 4 cups okra cut crosswise, fresh or frozen and slightly thawed, in a bowl with 1 cup cornmeal. Season with 1 teaspoon salt and ¼ teaspoon black pepper. Sauté in a heavy skillet with 4 tablespoons bacon drippings. This cooks in about 10 or 15 minutes. Use medium heat. Green tomatoes are also delicious cooked this way.

After a revival, a singing is held on a Saturday night and then a homecoming or reunion closes the service on Sunday, with more singing and dinner on the ground. These meals are quite elaborate sometimes, with the best foods, good tablecloths on the tables, and chairs to sit on.

Jessie's Pineapple Salad

(Very old recipe from relatives in North Carolina)

4 apples
1 20-ounce can pineapple chunks
1 3-ounce jar maraschino cherries
2 eggs

2 tablespoons sugar
2 tablespoons flour
1 16-ounce bag mini
   marshmallows

Cut fruit into very small pieces (by hand, not processor).

Beat 2 eggs, add sugar and flour, plus juice from pineapple and cherries. Cook over low heat until very thickened. Add ¾ bag marshmallows. Beat until smooth (by hand). Cool and pour over fruit. Add remaining marshmallows. Chill several hours or overnight. Keeps well in refrigerator. Recipe may be doubled if desired.

Fresh Green Beans

Wash beans carefully and cut or break in uniform lengths. Heat a tablespoon of bacon grease (this is proportion to use for about a half gallon of beans after they have been cut). Slice an onion in this hot grease and allow to cook for a few minutes. Add beans and a cup of hot water. Allow to simmer for 2 hours until tender. Then thicken this with a level tablespoon of cornstarch dissolved in 2 tablespoons water. Season with salt and pepper. (If desired seasoning can be added at first).

String Beans

Remove the strings from beans and wash in cold water. Cut or break into pieces about an inch long. Cook in boiling water until tender. Add salt a short time before the beans are tender. Drain and serve with butter, salt, and pepper or with a brown sauce.

*My mother's father, Grandpa Jake Owens, was a preacher,
a music teacher, and a schoolteacher.*

String Beans with Tomatoes

Melt two tablespoons butter and add 2 tablespoons flour and a cup of strained tomato juice. Make a smooth sauce of this and pour over the cooked string beans. Simmer for 15 minutes and serve hot.

Tomato Gravy

In pan where bacon, ham, or fatback has been cooked, drain all fat. Add back to pan:

5 or 6 tablespoons of grease	¼ teaspoon pepper
2 heaping tablespoons cornmeal	1 teaspoon beef bouillon
1 heaping tablespoon flour	2 cups tomato juice
1 teaspoon sugar	1 cup milk
¼ teaspoon salt	

Heat on medium heat until golden brown. Add the tomato juice and milk mixed. Cook until thick. Serve with bacon, corn bread, and fried potatoes.

BREADS

Hamburger Buns

1	cup milk	1⅓ cups unbleached white flour
1	teaspoon salt	⅔ cup whole wheat flour
3	tablespoons oil	2 tablespoons wheat germ
2	tablespoons sugar	Melted butter
1	package dry yeast	Sesame seeds (optional)

Scald milk. Add salt, oil, and sugar. Cool to lukewarm and pour over yeast. Add flours and wheat germ and mix well. Place on well-floured board and knead in additional white flour until dough is workable. Roll to about ½ inch thick on floured board and cut out buns approximately half the desired size. Place on greased cookie sheet. Brush tops with melted butter and sesame seeds and let rise about 1 hour. Bake 10 to 12 minutes at 350°. Makes 8 to 10 buns.

Hush Puppies

2	cups self-rising cornmeal	½ teaspoon pepper
1	egg, beaten	1 tablespoon sugar
1	small onion, chopped	Milk
½	teaspoon salt	Vegetable oil for frying

Mix together all ingredients except milk and oil. Add enough milk to make stiff batter. Drop by spoonfuls into skillet with hot oil. Fry until golden. Great with catfish.

Mother's Buttermilk Biscuits

· · · · · · · · · · · · · · · · · · · ·

2 cups self-rising flour
6 level teaspoons shortening
3 level teaspoons light margarine
(tub)

1 to 1⅓ cups buttermilk

Mix flour, shortening, and margarine together; add milk. Lay out aluminum foil on counter, put 2 tablespoons flour on foil; put the dough on it and knead by picking up and rolling with palm of hand. Take palm of hands or fingertips and spread out dough to fingertip thick; spread flour lightly over dough; then use biscuit cutter, drinking glass, or cup (dip in flour) to cut out the biscuits.

Knead remaining dough, sprinkle again with flour, and cut out biscuits. Lightly grease cookie sheet, put biscuits on sheet, rub tub butter or use squeeze butter on them, put in 400° to 425° oven, and bake 12 to 15 minutes. After about 5 minutes check bottom. When brown, crack oven door and turn on broil until tops turn brown.

To reheat, sprinkle a little water on biscuit, put in microwave, and heat for about 5 seconds.

Makes about 10 biscuits.

Biscuits with Cheese

· · · · · · · · · · · · · · · · · · · ·

½ pound sharp Cheddar cheese, grated
½ pound butter, softened
2 cups flour

Paprika
Powdered sugar
Almond slivers

Mix cheese and butter, mash, then cream thoroughly. Add flour to mixture and mix well. Add paprika for color. Shape into logs and chill. Slice thin and place on a lightly greased cookie sheet. Sprinkle with powdered sugar and center with almond slivers. Bake at 375° for 8 minutes. May be prepared in advance.

Mother's Tennessee Corn Bread

2 tablespoons bacon grease
1½ cups cornmeal
½ cup self-rising flour
   Pinch of baking soda
1 teaspoon baking powder
1 teaspoon salt
1 heaping tablespoon soft margarine
¾ cup buttermilk
   Cold water

Preheat oven to 450°.

Put 2 tablespoons bacon grease in a #8 iron skillet; set on stove on low heat, sprinkle a small amount of meal into it.

Mix all the dry ingredients together; blend in the margarine, add the buttermilk, stir. Add water until the batter is thin enough to pour from the mixing bowl. It will be slightly lumpy because of the margarine. Pour into the skillet, dip bacon grease from around the edges, and dribble it over the top. Put on lowest rack in the oven. Bake approximately 20 minutes; place under the broiler to brown the top well. Turn upside down onto a plate.

This singing group was from a school in Ivy Bluff in 1916. (Courtesy of Tennessee State Library and Archives)

Eggplant Pancakes

1   medium-size eggplant, peeled and
    sliced
¼   cup water

2   eggs
5   tablespoons flour
1   teaspoon salt

Bake eggplant with water, covered, at 350° until tender. Peel and remove seeds. Mash, add well-beaten eggs, flour, and salt. Mix all ingredients. Drop by spoonfuls on a hot buttered pan. Turn and brown on both sides.

Cornmeal Waffles

1   cup cornmeal
1   cup flour
4   teaspoons baking powder
4   tablespoons sugar

½   teaspoon salt
    Scant cup milk
2   well-beaten eggs
4   tablespoons melted fat

Mix and sift dry ingredients. Add milk gradually, then eggs and melted fat. Drop a tablespoon on each section of waffle iron. Bake until crisp and brown.

We never had a waffle iron. Our Aunt Estelle, Mother's older sister, did. She made these for us when we visited.

Blueberry Muffins

2   cups all-purpose flour
3   teaspoons baking powder
⅓   cup sugar
1   egg, beaten
1   cup milk

¼   cup vegetable oil
2   teaspoons lemon juice
1   cup fresh blueberries or ¾ cup
    frozen blueberries

Mix flour and baking powder and sugar. Set aside. Place egg in mixing bowl with milk. Add oil and lemon juice. Stir wet mixture with flour mixture. Blend in drained blueberries. Fill greased muffin tin ⅔ full. Bake 25 minutes at 350°. Makes 15 muffins.

DESSERTS AND SWEETS

Mary's Apple Dumplings

(Recipe over 100 years old)

Dough:
2 cups flour	Chilled water, as needed (as little
⅔ cup vegetable shortening	as possible)
¼ teaspoon salt	

Use pastry blender to cut flour, shortening, and salt into pie dough. Stir in water, a tablespoon at a time, until mixture forms a ball. Cover and chill slightly.

Filling:
5 apples, peeled and sliced	Cinnamon, nutmeg, sugar, grated
Raisins	lemon peel

Grease iron skillet. Divide dough into 6 to 8 rolls. Roll each out into circle. Place handful of apple slices, 1 tablespoon raisins, 1 teaspoon sugar, dash of cinnamon, nutmeg, and lemon on each circle. Stretch dough up over mixture and close on top. Carefully place in skillet.

Syrup:
1 cup sugar	Nutmeg
2 cups warm water	Raisins
Cinnamon	

Mix sugar and water. Add cinnamon, nutmeg, and raisins. Pour syrup over dumplings. Place butter pat on each. Bake at 400° for 10 minutes. Reduce to 350° for 30 to 40 minutes or until golden brown. Serve warm with milk poured over.

Black Raspberry Pie

5	cups black raspberries	⅓	cup flour
1	tablespoon orange juice	¼	teaspoon salt
1	cup sugar	2	pie shells, unbaked

Gently toss raspberries with orange juice and a mixture of other ingredients. Place filling in unbaked pie shell, heaping in center. Put top crust on. Bake at 450° for 10 minutes, then reduce heat to 350° and bake 25 to 30 minutes until done. Sweep top of pie with milk and sprinkle with white sugar.

Oatmeal Cake

1¼	cups boiling water	1	cup oatmeal

Stir oatmeal in water, let stand 20 minutes.

½	cup white sugar	2	eggs
½	cup brown sugar, packed	½	cup margarine or butter

Combine and beat well.

1½	cups flour	1	teaspoon baking soda
½	teaspoon salt	1	teaspoon cinnamon

Blend in oatmeal. Add dry ingredients and mix. Bake in 9x11-inch pan at 350° for 35 minutes.

After people became Christians, they would be baptised. Unless they belonged to a really big church, the baptism would usually be in a creek like this one up in Carter County. (Courtesy of Tennessee State Library and Archives)

Honey Cake

½ cup shortening	1 teaspoon baking powder
1 cup honey	¼ teaspoon salt
1 egg, well beaten	½ teaspoon cinnamon
2 cups flour	½ cup sour milk or buttermilk

Cream shortening. Add honey and egg. Sift flour; measure and sift with baking powder, salt, and cinnamon. Add milk to first mixture. Mix all thoroughly. Pour into shallow, well-oiled 9x9-inch pan. Bake at 350° for 50 minutes.

Pineapple Casserole

6 tablespoons butter or margarine
6 slices bread, cubed
2 beaten eggs
½ cup sugar
2 tablespoons flour
1 20-ounce can crushed pineapple

Melt butter in a large skillet (iron works best). Add bread cubes and brown slightly. Add eggs, sugar, and flour to pineapple and mix all ingredients lightly in skillet. Turn into buttered casserole and bake at 375° for about 40 minutes, until just firm. Serve warm.

Coconut Pie

2 cups milk
¾ cup sugar
½ cup Bisquick mix
4 eggs
¼ cup butter
½ teaspoon vanilla extract
1 cup coconut

Combine milk, sugar, ½ cup coconut, Bisquick, eggs, butter, and vanilla in electric blender. Cover and blend on low speed for 3 minutes. Pour into greased 9-inch pie pan. Let stand 5 minutes. Sprinkle with ½ cup coconut. Bake at 350° for 40 minutes. Serve hot or cold.

Pudding Cake

1 14-ounce can Eagle Brand sweetened condensed milk
¼ cup lemon juice
1 12-ounce bowl Cool Whip
1 20-ounce can crushed pineapple, drained
1 box vanilla wafers
9 bananas, sliced

Mix first four ingredients thoroughly. Layer bananas and wafers, cover with pudding mixture. Keep layering until all mixture is gone, then crush wafers on top.

Mother's Banana Pudding

3	pounds bananas, sliced	3	whole eggs
2	large boxes Nilla Wafers	1	stick butter
1	cup sugar		Dash salt
½	cup flour	6	cups milk
6	egg yolks (set aside egg whites for meringue topping)	2	teaspoons vanilla extract

Place sliced bananas and vanilla wafers in a large pan. Mix together sugar, flour, egg yolks, eggs, butter, and salt. Add the milk, a little at a time. Cook slowly until the mixture thickens. Let it cool for a few minutes, then add vanilla. Pour over bananas and vanilla wafers.

Meringue Topping:

6	egg whites	1	tablespoon sugar
1	teaspoon lemon juice	1	teaspoon vanilla extract

Beat the 6 egg whites with 1 teaspoon lemon juice, 1 tablespoon sugar, and 1 teaspoon vanilla until stiff. Spoon this mixture over the top of the pudding and brown in the oven.

In the fifties and sixties, we sometimes could buy bananas to make banana pudding—in a dishpan (a white enamel pan). We rinsed dishes in it, made corn bread in it, and we had always made the snow cream in it. Mother used a pan the size of the aluminum washpan for biscuits, but it was white with a red rim. I remember the biscuit pan had a couple of chips knocked out of the bottom and a small hole in it. Mother had put a piece of cloth through it to patch it. She kept it full of flour with an indent in it where she would put salt, lard, soda, baking powder, and milk—just enough to make the amount of biscuits we needed. Then she would roll the dough in her hands, place it in a pan, and put it in the stove to bake. She always refilled the pan with flour, made the hole in the center, and covered it with a towel (made from a cloth sack). Then she would put it into the cabinet until the next meal.

Fudge Frosting

9 ounces semisweet chocolate bits
2 tablespoons butter, melted
1 cup sifted powdered sugar

¼ cup hot milk
1 teaspoon vanilla extract

Melt chocolate and butter together over hot water. Stir until smooth. Add sifted powdered sugar alternately with hot milk; add vanilla and beat until smooth and satiny and just right for spreading.

My son, Mitchell Blalock, and his wife, Kathy.

Company for Easter Dinner

Do you know when Easter will be each year? It's the first Sunday, after the first full moon, after the vernal equinox, which is the official first day of spring. Now, isn't that something? We always just called it "Spring of the Year."

As much as I enjoy autumn and the real pleasures of winter, I do look forward to spring too. Spring in the hills and mountains is truly glorious—a really special time. It's always interesting to me to see the cars lined up bumper to bumper going into the Smokies in the spring, carrying folks to see the wild flowers. We grew up with them, and I don't know what we kids would have thought of thousands of people getting that excited about something we loved but that was an everyday— at least in the spring—part of our lives.

In the spring, we couldn't wait to get our gardens out. We put potatoes and onions and cabbage in the ground as early as March. We covered the tender plants with anything we could find—canvas, cheesecloth, glass jars—to protect them from late frosts. Then we had to hurry in the mornings and uncover them before the sun got warm and they got "scalded." All of us were involved in the gardens, and it wouldn't be long before we had fresh lettuce and onions and radishes and the like.

We picked "poke salad" all spring. We cooked it and fried it. We started frying green tomatoes when they got about the size of tennis balls.

We had wonderfully sweet strawberries growing wild in our mountains, as well as "mountain tea berries." There were not enough for pies or cakes—just enough for "treats."

In the South, Easter dinner used to be just as important as Thanksgiving or Christmas dinner. Usually the best ham had been saved for the occasion. At our house it was the pork shoulder. Papa always sold the hams because that was extra money for the household. The tenderest, youngest vegetables that we might have available—depending on how late that full moon came—were cooked to go along with it. I remember the house filled with the rich, inviting aroma of hot yeast rolls—a very special treat. Since there weren't many fruits yet for pies, cakes were usually the dessert for this dinner.

In keeping with our awareness of the meaning of Easter for Christians, we regarded this important family gathering—which was usually the first since the long winter—as a signal of renewal. Spring began a long season of hard work for farmers, and that, too, lent special meaning to this gathering when we feasted on the last of the previous year's bounty and the first of this year's. And the thread that always ran through these gatherings was the constancy of family and the strength we all took from that.

MAIN DISHES

Quick Chicken Casserole

Cook stew chicken and take off bones. Place in oblong pan. Pour 1 can cream of chicken soup over chicken. Soften 1 package stuffing mix with chicken broth and spread over chicken. Bake at 350° until brown. Serve.

Chicken Stew

3 to 4 pounds chicken	¼ teaspoon celery salt
Boiling water	2 tablespoons butter
1 teaspoon salt	½ cup flour
1 teaspoon pepper	

Wash chicken carefully, cut into pieces, cover with boiling water, cook until tender. Add salt, pepper, and celery salt when chicken is half cooked. Blend butter, flour, add a little cold water to make a smooth paste, add to chicken about 10 minutes before ready to serve.

Chicken Livers

2 pounds chicken livers	10 slices bacon, fried well done and
1 medium onion, chopped fine	crumbled
1 tablespoon butter	2 tablespoons mayonnaise
2 hard-boiled eggs, crumbled	1 teaspoon black pepper

Fry livers and onion in butter until livers are cooked through. Add chopped eggs, crumbled bacon, mayonnaise, and pepper. Mix well. Serve cold with crackers.

Chicken Pot Pie

. . . .

1   chicken, cooked, skinned, and
    deboned
1½ cups chicken broth

1   10¾-ounce can cream of chicken
    soup

Cut chicken into small pieces. Put in a casserole dish. Combine soup and broth and pour over chicken.

Topping:

1   cup plain flour
2   teaspoons baking powder
1   teaspoon salt

½   teaspoon black pepper
1   cup milk
1   stick margarine, melted

For the topping, mix dry ingredients with milk and margarine and pour over top. Bake at 350° for about 35 minutes or until brown.

Rice Stuffing for Chicken

. . . .

1¼ cups uncooked rice
2   medium onions, chopped
1   cup celery, chopped
½   cup butter
½   teaspoon salt

½   teaspoon pepper
½   teaspoon garlic powder
    Giblets, cooked and chopped
    (reserve 1 cup cooking liquid)

Cook rice as directed on package. Sauté onions and celery in butter; add rice, salt, pepper, garlic powder, and cooked giblets. Add 1 cup cooking liquid from giblets and mix well. Stuff chicken and bake. If desired as a side dish, place mixture in a casserole dish and bake for approximately 20 to 25 minutes at 350°.

Fried Roasted Steak

2	2-inch thick round steaks	2	cans mushroom soup or golden
	Salt		mushroom soup
	Celery salt	1	onion, chopped
	Pepper	4	potatoes, sliced
	Flour	3	large carrots, diced
2	tablespoons oil or butter		

Season steak with salt, celery salt, and pepper; then pound flour into steak. Brown meat in hot oil, place in roaster pan, pour cans of soup over meat, and simmer 1½ hours. Cover meat with chopped onion, sliced potatoes, and diced carrots. Cook another hour. Serve with bread and salad.

Country Ham Cooked in Milk

Sliced country ham	Dry mustard
Brown sugar	Whole milk, to cover ham

Slice ham ½ to ¾ inch thick. Mix brown sugar and mustard, rub on both sides of ham slices. Place slices in baking dish. Pour milk over ham. Bake uncovered at 325° about 2½ hours or until tender. Serve with milk sauce over ham slices.

Apples and Country Ham

4	slices of country ham (sliced thick)	4	apples, peeled, cored, and sliced
3	tablespoons butter	2	tablespoons brown sugar

Fry ham in butter until brown, take out of pan, add apples to pan and brown. Put ham back in pan, add brown sugar, cover, and simmer until heated to boiling point, about 7 minutes. Serve hot.

Salmon Loaf

. . . .

(I always double this.)

1	15-ounce can salmon	1	tablespoon butter
1	cup soda biscuits rolled fine or breadcrumbs	2	teaspoon onion, chopped fine
1	cup milk	1	teaspoon lemon juice,
½	teaspoon salt	1	egg

Preheat oven to 400° (or 350° if using glass baking dish). Mix salmon and crumbs. Add remaining ingredients.

Mix well and put in loaf pan. Bake about 45 minutes.

Grits and Cheese Casserole

. . . .

1	cup grits	3	cups grated sharp cheese
1	teaspoon salt	1	egg, beaten
4	cups water	1	cup milk
1	stick margarine		

Cook grits, salt, and water according to directions on box. Add margarine, cheese, beaten egg, and milk. Place in buttered baking dish. Bake at 350° for 20 to 30 minutes.

Chicken Salad

. . . .

	Meat from 1 cooked chicken, skinned, deboned, and chopped		Juice of ½ lemon
1	cup celery, chopped fine	1	cup mayonnaise or salad dressing
½	cup sweet pickles, chopped fine		Salt and pepper

Mix well. Keep in refrigerator.

VEGETABLES AND SIDE DISHES

Corn with Cheese

4 eggs	½ teaspoon paprika
1½ tablespoons butter	2 cups milk
1 15-ounce can whole kernel corn	½ cup grated cheese
½ teaspoon salt	1 cup cracker crumbs
Pepper	

Beat eggs, add butter melted over hot water. Add to corn, then add seasonings. Add milk and mix well. Add grated cheese. Fill buttered baking dish half full and cover with half the crumbs, add remaining corn mixture, then crumbs, and bake in 350° oven until firm, about 30 to 40 minutes.

Fried Poke Stalks

Gather a large bunch of poke stalks, skin the pink and green skin off as much as possible. Slice, boil a few minutes, drain, and rinse in cool water. Dip in beaten egg batter, then in meal and flour mixture. Fry in hot oil or bacon grease.

Fried Poke Salad

Cook 2 pounds poke greens, leaves and young stalks. (Pick when about 3 or 4 inches tall.) Drain and rinse after cooked. Heat an iron skillet with grease or oil. Add greens and 3 beaten eggs, salt, and pepper to taste.

We gathered watercress as well as dry-land cress. We cooked both with salt and bacon grease. We ate the watercress raw and cooked. We used the early turnip and mustard and poke salad greens also.

My sister Rachel (second from the left) *is with some of our cousins at a family reunion in the mid 1980s.*

Creamed Poke Salad

Gather a large bunch of poke greens (3 or 4 bunches or 2 cans of poke salad greens).

If greens are fresh, cook about 20 minutes. Drain and rinse with cold water.

3 or 4 ham hocks	5 tablespoons flour
2 cups water	2 cups cream
4 tablespoons butter	Boil meat in 4 cups water until very

tender, take off of the bone. Add greens to ham, add 2 cups water, and simmer 30 minutes. Drain off extra water, melt butter in a skillet, add flour, stirring. Add cream, cook until thick sauce stage. Add greens and ham. This is good made with spinach also.

Curried Eggs

4 eggs	1 teaspoon curry powder
3 tablespoons cream	2 tablespoons cooking fat
½ teaspoon salt	8 thin slices dried beef
⅓ teaspoon pepper	4 slices bread

Beat eggs well. Add cream and seasonings. Heat cooking fat in frying pan. Add eggs. Cook slowly, stirring constantly until of creamy consistency. Pile in center of serving platter. Border with toast fingers and dried beef curls, which have been browned in butter. Serve hot.

Our grandparents had an old metal-and-wood icebox with a large block of ice in it. I would watch in fascination while the iceman with the ice tongs and a burlap sack put a new block of ice in the box. Grandma Rena would clean the box with soda water and dry it. It had a drain for the melted ice to drip out into a bucket.

We had Grandma's old one for a while, but the iceman didn't come into the mountains where we lived at Locust Ridge, which is now Dolly's Tennessee mountain home.

I don't remember what happened to that icebox. We used a spring house when we lived there, and when we moved from there we had a round wash tub at the well to catch water from a hand pump. In cool weather, Mother would make Jell-O, chocolate milk, and pudding and put them in the cold water, to keep cold along with the milk and butter. If we had food left over (beans, potatoes, peas, or gravy), it was put in a jar with a lid and placed there until the next day.

Milk Gravy or Soup

Made like red-eye gravy except use milk, not coffee or water. We ate this with corn bread on cold winter evenings for dinner sometimes.

Just fry ham, bacon, or side meat until brown. Pour off all fat, add a dash of salt and pepper to hot pan. Pour 3 cups of milk in pan and heat to boiling. Add 1 cup whole kernel corn. Serve hot in cups or bowls with corn bread and ham or bacon. I serve this as a light soup before dinner when I have company.

Fried Potatoes (Taters)

You first buy some taters—I know you will never grow them—then you peel them and wash them and then you slice them and then you put lard, butter, or oil in the skillet and let it get hot and then you put the taters in that and fry until done. (If you can keep your husband out of them, you will have supper cooked.)

—Given to a new bride at her wedding shower

111111111111111111

Boiled Cabbage

Wash the cabbage in cold water and remove wilted leaves. Cut into quarters and cover with boiling salted water. Boil until tender. Add a strip of fried bacon, or a spoonful of bacon grease while cabbage is boiling for flavor. Drain, sprinkle with salt and pepper, and heat with 2 tablespoons of butter. Serve hot. Red cabbage may be prepared in the same way but the water must be changed 4 times to destroy the strong taste.

Banana Salad

1 egg, beaten	¾ cup sugar
2 tablespoons cider vinegar	1 tablespoon flour
1¼ cups water	3 bananas, peeled and sliced

Mix egg, vinegar, and water. Stir well. Blend in sugar and flour. Cook until thick. Stir constantly. Cool. Place bananas in serving platter. Cover with sauce and serve.

Fried Black-Eyed Peas

2 cups cooked black-eyed peas	1 teaspoon salt
1 cup cooked smoked ham, finely chopped	¼ teaspoon pepper
½ cup corn flakes, finely crushed	1 egg, separated
1½ teaspoons onion, grated	¾ cup flour
1½ teaspoons fresh parsley, finely chopped	¼ cup milk
	2 cups corn flakes, finely crushed
	Tomato sauce (optional)

Mash the peas until soft. Add ham, ½ cup corn flakes, onion, parsley, salt, pepper, and egg yolk. Mix thoroughly. Using generous tablespoons of mixture, form into balls. Coat with flour. Beat egg white slightly with milk. Roll the mixture in this, then in the remaining corn flakes. Fry in deep fat and brown both sides. Drain on paper towel. Serve with warm tomato sauce if desired. Serves 4 to 6.

Grandpa Jim and Grandma Melinda Owens were Grandpa Jake's (see page 16) parents. In this picture, taken on their farm in the early 1930s, I think they are trying to decide whether to have chicken and dumplings or roast duck.

Cornmeal Dumplings

1   cup cornmeal
¼   teaspoon black pepper

¼   teaspoon red pepper
    Ham stock

Mix meal and spices Have ham stock boiling. Pour 1 cup boiling stock over meal mixture and stir into dough stiff enough to drop from spoon, in balls about the size of an egg. Drop in briskly boiling stock, then turn heat low. Simmer about 20 minutes. Any stock can be used (beef, ham, vegetable). Serve as a side dish or the bread for the meal.

Hot Slaw

1 medium head cabbage	1 teaspoon vinegar
1 cup milk	Salt to taste
1 tablespoon butter	Paprika to taste
3 or 4 egg yolks	Pepper to taste

Shred cabbage and place in ice water to crisp. Heat milk in double boiler, add butter and egg yolks. Stir and cook until thickened. When cool, add a little vinegar, mix well with drained cabbage, add seasoning.

Kraut Slaw

1 quart kraut, drained	1 cup sugar
1 cup chopped green bell peppers	½ cup vinegar
1 cup chopped onion	

Mix all together and put in refrigerator. Will keep for a long time. Add hot pepper if you like it hot!

Spiced Apple and Cornmeal Pudding

1 cup yellow cornmeal	2 eggs, beaten
4 cups milk	3 tablespoons butter
⅔ cup molasses	½ teaspoon salt
1 cup diced apples	½ teaspoon cinnamon
½ cup sugar	½ teaspoon nutmeg

Add meal to milk and cook, stirring until thick. Let cool; add other ingredients. Put in a buttered baking dish and bake 1 hour and 45 minutes at 325°. Serve with whipped cream or ice cream.

In 1910 most people made their own butter by churning it. (Courtesy of Tennessee State Library and Archives)

Churning was everybody's job. When the cream came to the top of the milk that was fermented, it made a good tasting butter when it was churned—more of an aged taste that we preferred, not as sweet as the fresh cream. The butter was washed in cold water and lightly salted, formed into a ball, and put into a butter dish.

Fried Beets

Wash six large beets and boil them until soft. Then peel them and chop them up fine. Cut up 3 slices bacon in small pieces, and fry until crisp. Add the chopped beets and fry. Put the beets to one side and add 2 tablespoons vinegar and bring to a boil, then add 1 tablespoon sugar and mix. Sprinkle 1 tablespoon flour over the beets and season to taste.

Scattered Potatoes

Shred 3 or 4 medium potatoes, using coarse side of vegetable cutter, the one for cabbage. Add salt, pepper, a generous dash of garlic, parsley flakes, and a tablespoon of flour. Mix all into potatoes, fry in hot oil.

Boiled Beets

Wash but do not cut beets, only cut off the green tops. Cook in boiling water until tender. Beets take a very long time to cook. When thoroughly cooked, drain, and pour on cold water. This will loosen the skins so they may be rubbed off. Serve young beets with melted butter, salt, and pepper. (Remember, beet juice will stain your hands.)

Carrots and Peas

Wash, scrape, and dice the carrots. Cook in salted water until tender. Drain canned or cooked fresh peas and mix with carrots. Sprinkle with about 2 tablespoons flour, add 2 tablespoons butter, season, and add ½ cup soup stock. Boil a little longer and serve. Carrots and peas may also be served with a creamed sauce. A little sugar may also be added.

Our favorite school lunch, when we started getting them at school, was meatloaf, creamed potatoes, peas, a slice of white loaf bread, and half of a canned peach or oatmeal cookies for dessert.

Mashed Potatoes

. . . .

6   hot cooked potatoes
6   tablespoons hot milk
3   tablespoons butter

1   teaspoon salt
    Pepper

Mash the potatoes until free from any lumps. Add the hot milk, butter, and then salt and pepper. Beat with a fork to make creamy and fluffy. Reheat and serve in a hot dish, garnish with parsley, and dot with butter.

Taken in the early 1950s at Aunt Estelle's house is this picture of front (left to right): *Dwight Puckett, Cassie, and Randy;* middle (left to right): *Stella, Dale Puckett, Denver, Dolly, Donna Faye Puckett, and Bobby;* back: *David and me (Willadeene). The Pucketts were our cousins.*

Wilted Lettuce Salad

....

1   large bowl leaf lettuce, cut up
4   to 6 green onions, cut up (blades
    and all)

¼   cup cider vinegar
6   to 8 slices bacon

Mix the lettuce, onions, and vinegar. Fry the slices of bacon and pour hot grease onto salad. Sprinkle bits of bacon over the top of salad, if you wish. Toss and serve at once. Serves 8 to 10.

We planted rows of the cane seed each spring—seed that Papa and Mother had carefully dried and taken care of through the winter. I remember how the round cane and okra seeds would roll off the ends of my fingers into the rich dark mountain dirt that Papa made shallow furrows in. We truly did eat bread by the sweat of our brow . . . along with many other foods.

DESSERTS AND SWEETS

Strawberry and Peach Dream Cake

....

1½ cups self-rising flour
½   cup sugar
½   cup (1 stick) butter, softened
1   egg, beaten
½   cup milk

Topping:
1   cup minced fresh strawberries
1½ cups sliced fresh peaches
½   cup sugar
½   teaspoon cinnamon
3   tablespoons melted butter

Preheat oven to 350°. Grease 13x9x2-inch glass baking dish, set aside. Prepare cake batter by combining flour and sugar in large mixing bowl. Cut in butter with a pastry blender or fork, until mixture resembles coarse crumbs. Stir in egg and milk until just blended. Spread batter evenly in prepared pan. Bake 30 to 35 minutes or until a toothpick inserted in the middle comes out clean. While cake is still warm, prepare topping.

For topping, arrange sliced fruit in rows over cake. Combine sugar and cinnamon. Sprinkle evenly over fruit. Drizzle with melted butter. Serve warm or at room temperature. Serves 8.

Key Lime Pie

1	tablespoon unflavored gelatin	⅛	teaspoon green food coloring
¼	teaspoon salt	½	cup sugar
½	cup lime juice	2	cups whipped topping
½	cup sugar	1	9-inch graham cracker pie crust, chilled
4	eggs, separated		
¼	cup water		

In a saucepan blend gelatin, salt, lime juice, ½ cup sugar, egg yolks, and water; mix well. Cook and stir over medium heat just to boiling. Remove from heat and stir in food coloring. Chill until partially set. Beat egg whites until soft peaks are formed. Add ½ cup sugar and beat until stiff peaks are formed. Fold into gelatin mixture. Prepare whipped topping and fold into pie mixture. Pour into chilled pie shell. Chill until firm. Garnish with whipped topping and lime slices.

Rice Pudding

⅓	cup raw rice	½	teaspoon nutmeg or 1 teaspoon vanilla extract
5	cups milk		
⅓	cup sugar	½	teaspoon salt

Mix in baking dish and bake at 300° for 1½ hours or more. Stir every 20 minutes or so. You can add ¾ cup raisins the last half hour of baking.

Lemon Meringue Pie

1 cup sugar
6 tablespoons cornstarch (if it doesn't thicken, add more as needed)
1 cup boiling water

Juice and grated rind of 3 lemons
1 teaspoon butter (optional)
2 eggs, separated
1 baked pie shell or 1 graham cracker shell

Mix sugar and cornstarch in saucepan and stir in boiling water. Cook, stirring, until thick; stir in lemon juice, lemon rind, and butter. Blend in beaten egg yolks; pour into baked pie shell. Beat egg whites until foamy and add sugar to taste. Beat until stiff. Spread on top of pie. Bake at 350° to 375° until top browns (quickly).

You can't mess this up. I usually just throw it all together and triple the recipe for more pies. You can make three just as quickly as you can make one.

Lemon Cheesecake

1 3-ounce package lemon Jell-O
3 tablespoons lemon juice
1 8-ounce package cream cheese
1 cup sugar
1 teaspoon vanilla extract
1 cup chilled prepared whipped topping

1 cup melted butter or margarine (may need more to hold crust together)
1 pound graham crackers, crushed

Dissolve Jell-O in boiling water; add lemon juice and cool.

Cream together cheese, sugar, and vanilla. Add to Jell-O and mix well. Fold in whipped topping.

Mix butter and crumbs. Line bottom and sides of a 13x9x2-inch pan. Add filling and sprinkle top with some of the crumbs.

Chill. Serves 12 to 16.

White Bread Pudding

2 cups stale breadcrumbs	4 eggs
1 pint cream or milk	¼ teaspoon cinnamon
½ cup sugar	Salt
4 tablespoons melted butter	½ teaspoon vanilla extract

Soak breadcrumbs in cream. Add sugar, butter, beaten eggs, cinnamon, salt, and flavoring. Place in buttered baking dish and place in a pan of hot water. Bake in slow oven, 300° to 325°, about 35 minutes. Serve with a pinch of grated orange peel, chopped raisins, dates, and cream.

Hot Fudge Chocolate Sauce

1 cup brown sugar	1 tablespoon butter
½ cup water	½ teaspoon vanilla
4 tablespoons cocoa	

Blend sugar, water, and cocoa, dissolved in a little boiling water. Boil together 5 minutes. Cool and add butter and vanilla.

Caramel Frosting

2 cups brown sugar	½ teaspoon vanilla extract or maple flavoring
½ cup butter	
3 tablespoons cream	½ cup shredded coconut

Cook together sugar, butter, and cream until quite thick. Beat thoroughly. Add vanilla and shredded coconut. Half a cup of nut meats, chopped, may be added.

Mother was the middle of three sisters. Aunt Estelle (shown here with her husband, Uncle Dot, and Dolly) was the oldest; Aunt Dorothy Jo was the youngest.

Pineapple Upside Down Cake

⅓	cup butter	⅓	teaspoon salt
⅔	cup sugar	⅔	cup water
2	eggs, separated	4	tablespoons butter
½	teaspoon vanilla	1	cup brown sugar
1½	cups flour		*Canned or fresh fruit: pineapple,*
3	teaspoons baking powder		*peach, or apricot may be used*

Cream ⅓ cup butter, add ⅔ cup sugar, beaten egg yolks, and vanilla. Sift together flour, baking powder, salt; add to first mixture alternately with water. Fold in stiffly beaten egg whites. While making cake batter, melt 4 tablespoons butter and brown sugar. When thick add cut pineapple or halves of ripe peaches or apricots. Pour batter over fruit and bake about 35 minutes in 350° oven. Remove to dish, turning upside down so that the fruit will be on top. Serve hot with hard sauce or whipped cream.

Heavenly Cake

1   box of cake mix, any brand
    Add ½ cup water over what cake
    mix calls for
1   cup finely chopped nuts

4   heaping tablespoons self-rising
    flour
⅓   stick butter, melted
½   cup brown sugar, firmly packed

Mix ingredients thoroughly.

Bake as directed on package or until toothpick comes out clean when inserted. Ice with caramel frosting (recipe on page 45), or serve warm.

Fudge Sauce

1   cup sugar
6   tablespoons cocoa

½   cup cream
½   teaspoon vanilla extract

Boil sugar, cocoa, cream to form soft ball when tested in cold water. Add vanilla. Beat when cool.

Malted Milk Cake

⅔   cup butter or margarine
1   cup sugar
2   eggs, well beaten
2½ cups cake flour

3   teaspoons baking powder
⅓   cup malted milk powder
¼   teaspoon salt
1   cup milk

Cream butter or margarine with sugar. Add eggs. Mix thoroughly. Sift flour, measure, and sift with baking powder, malted milk powder, and salt. Add alternately with milk to first mixture. Mix thoroughly. Pour into well-greased layer cake pans. Bake at 350° for 30 to 35 minutes.

Raspberry or Blackberry Jam Cake with Boiled Frosting

⅔	cup butter	1	teaspoon baking soda
1	cup sugar	1	teaspoon cinnamon
1	cup jam without seeds	¼	cup buttermilk or sour cream
3	eggs, separated	1	teaspoon vanilla or lemon extract
2½	cups pastry flour		

Cream butter and sugar. Add jam to egg yolks, mix together, add to butter and sugar. Sift dry ingredients together and add alternately with buttermilk. Fold in beaten egg whites, add vanilla, bake in butter-lined pans in 350° oven, top with boiled frosting or brown sugar frosting for filling of cake, when cool.

Hannah Dennison (my sister Rachel's daughter) and Rebecca Seaver (my sister Cassie's daughter) joined me for lunch in Nashville after an autograph party for Smoky Mountain Memories.

Boiled Frosting with Corn Syrup

2   cups granulated sugar
¼   cup white corn syrup
6   tablespoons water
2   egg whites

1   tablespoon vanilla, lemon, or
    almond extract
½   cup shredded coconut or chopped
    nuts

Boil sugar, syrup, and water together until soft-ball stage in cold water. Slowly pour mixture into stiffly beaten egg whites, beating constantly. Add flavoring, beat until quite cool. Chopped nuts or shredded coconut may be used for filling. Frosting may be kept several days if poured in glass jar and placed in refrigerator. When ready to use place bowl in pan of hot water, then beat. Toasted coconut is good with this.

Brown Sugar Frosting

1   stick butter
1   cup brown sugar

1   small can evaporated milk
1   box powdered sugar

Cook butter and brown sugar until caramelized. Add milk, let boil for about 5 minutes or more. Pour into bowl that powdered sugar has been added to. Use mixer and add hot water—a few drops at a time—until smooth and creamy. Frost cake.

Baked Custard

3   eggs
2   cups milk
¼   cup sugar

¼   teaspoon salt
½   teaspoon vanilla

Beat eggs only until blended. Mix in milk, sugar, salt, and vanilla.
    Pour into baking dish and set in a pan of water. Bake for 60 minutes or until firm at 350°. Do not overcook.

Hummingbird Pie

⅓ cup lemon juice
1 14-ounce can sweetened
condensed milk
2 or 3 ripe bananas, sliced
1 9-inch graham cracker crust

1 8-ounce can crushed pineapple
½ cup pecan pieces
1 8-ounce carton whipped topping
½ cup coconut
Maraschino cherries

Combine lemon juice and condensed milk, stir until thick. Place bananas in the bottom of pie crust. Spread milk and lemon juice mixture evenly over bananas. Drain pineapple some, but not until dry. Spread pineapple and half of the pecans over banana-milk layer. Spread whipped topping evenly over the top. Refrigerate. When ready to serve, garnish with remaining pecans, coconut, and cherries. Refrigerate leftovers.

3

Visitation Days and Caton's Chapel Decoration-Day Picnic

In the introduction to this book, I spoke about how nothing moved a southern cook into the kitchen faster than a death in the family or community. And that is true.

Now, I know that we southerners are not the only ones who gather together in this way or in ways similar to this—take the legendary Irish wakes for instance. And, of course, a lot of the hill and mountain folk throughout southern Appalachia are of Irish descent or "Scotch-Irish" as some used to be called when I was growing up. I guess some of the tradition comes from that culture. I was grown before I found out that being part "Scotch-Irish" didn't mean that you were part Irish and part Scot but that you were "Irish Protestant" rather than "Irish Catholic."

I guess one of the ways many of us deal with death—especially when it is a relative or friend or neighbor—is to try to reaffirm "life." And one of the best ways to do that—I think—is the old-fashioned southern tradition of "Visitation." The "dearly departed" is laid out in one room. Gathered around are relatives, friends, and neighbors telling stories—usually happy or funny ones—that recall the dead. I mean that literally. Those stories call back the spirit of the person who has passed to refresh our memories of that person's life and how it touched ours.

Because these events were usually a gathering of folks who had grown up together, worked together, eaten together, lived together for at least parts of their lives, invariably the dishes that were brought and laid out in another room evoked memories of past times and gatherings when the person whose passing we had come to acknowledge was still with us. In this way, while mourning went on, these gatherings were also a celebration of the person's life. And that's mighty important. The "Visitation" came to emphasize the continuity of life, and the food that was an integral part of that gathering was also an integral part of that process. To put it plainly, a dish of butter beans or a buttermilk pie or a bowl of potato salad that someone has taken the time and effort to prepare and bring says more about love and caring and sympathy than the grandest spray of flowers or the sweetest sympathy card ever can.

A lot of people outside the South don't know about "Decoration Day." It is in May. Originally—at least in most parts of the South—it was on "Confederate Memorial Day." Families would go to the local cemetery to "decorate" the graves of their family members who were killed during the "War of Northern Aggression."

Of course, east Tennessee has a somewhat different tradition because east Tennessee was never a staunch supporter of the Confederacy. In fact, Confederate troops were sent into parts of east Tennessee to put down rebellion against the rebellion. Remember, Lincoln's second vice-president, Andrew Johnson, was from east Tennessee.

Anyway, now, throughout most of the South, decoration day is usually observed on Memorial Day at the end of May. It is still a day to "decorate" graves of loved ones—often those killed during one war or another. It is also a day when families gather together to eat and remember those who have passed on, as well as just to "re-convene" families who no longer all live in one valley or one town or now even one state.

As with other southern "gathering" times, each cook would bring her favorite or best dish. Sometimes, different parts of families would "save up" their resources so that they could bring a dish they could be proud of. More often, though, there was a recognition among all that the "widow's mite" was more valued than the fanciest dish of a city cousin.

The dishes were prepared from the foods of spring. One uncle would slaughter a young cow and aunt would then bring a platter of "country-fried" steak. For those of you who don't know, "country-fried" steak is different from "chicken-fried" steak. Both dishes generally start with slices of some of the perhaps less tender pieces of beef—usually a half inch or less thick. Chicken-fried steak is then breaded, as you would chicken for fried chicken, and it is pan fried, again, as you would chicken. Country-fried steak, on the other hand is also pan fried, usually beginning with a little fatback or bacon grease. Then, as the steak cooks, you make gravy in the pan as you go and finish the cooking of the meat in the gravy and serve it with the gravy in which it cooked.

So, if someone tries to sell you a "country-fried" steak sandwich that is really chicken-fried steak on a bun—don't buy it if you really want country-fried steak. Fix your own.

Some families would go to the cemetery in the morning, then gather for their meal in the afternoon. Others would eat lunch, then gather at the cemetery in the afternoon. Often, these meals—whenever they were—might be called "picnics," but that doesn't fairly describe them. Tables were set up—often boards on sawhorses—tablecloths spread, and the tables covered with a wonderful array of dishes: hams, roasts, potato salads, pole beans, field peas, creamed corn, fried okra, butter beans, pies, cakes, puddings, fresh rolls and biscuits, tomatoes. I've made myself hungry just thinking about it.

As I think back on some of those days, on the loved ones passed on and those still with us, on the love and care that went into the preparation of those meals, and the spirit of the gathering together, a phrase comes into my thoughts. Those special days were a "communion of saints." Our meal was to celebrate the memory of those who were no longer with us and to celebrate our own gathering together in their memory. Decoration Day is decorated in my heart and my memory with pictures of my family.

MAIN DISHES

Hot Chicken

1 fryer, cut up
1 cup chopped celery
½ cup Louisiana Hot Sauce
½ cup water
3 tablespoons garlic powder

Preheat oven to 375°.

Place chicken pieces in a shallow pan. Sprinkle on celery. Mix hot sauce with water in measuring cup and pour over chicken. Sprinkle on garlic powder, place in oven. Bake until brown. Lower heat to 300° and cover chicken with aluminum foil. Bake another 30 minutes or until meat is tender. Serves 4 to 6. This same method can be used for pork chops.

Southern Fried Chicken

10 to 12 pieces of fresh chicken
    (never frozen)
2 cups buttermilk (to tenderize and
    flavor)
    Lard or oil
1 tablespoon bacon grease (for
    flavor)
2 cups flour
2½ teaspoons salt
1½ teaspoons pepper

Wash chicken in cold water, dry with towels, place in a large bowl, and add buttermilk. Turn all pieces to coat with buttermilk and place in refrigerator for 1 hour.

Chicken is crispiest when fried in 2 inches of oil. Heat oil to 350°. This is the right temperature to brown the outside while sealing moisture inside. Bacon grease can be added at this time to add flavor.

Remove chicken from buttermilk and dredge in mixture of flour, salt, and pepper. Place in hot oil, cover. Chicken should be turned just once while cooking. Fry 10 to 12 minutes.

Quick Spaghetti

Spaghetti
2 medium-size onions, chopped
½ teaspoon pepper
1 1-pint can of tomatoes

½ teaspoon parsley, chopped
½ teaspoon salt
2 teaspoons sugar
½ cup grated sharp Cheddar cheese

Cook spaghetti in salted water. Cook onions and pepper in olive oil until half tender. Add canned tomatoes, parsley, salt, and sugar. Cook very slowly until onions are tender. Turn cooked spaghetti into warmed dish, stir cheese into sauce, pour sauce over spaghetti, and serve hot. Serve additional dry grated cheese in a side dish.

This tent revival, held by Ashley and Emma Johnson at Johnson Bible College, is just like the tent revivals Grandpa Jake used to hold throughout east Tennessee. (Courtesy of Johnson Bible College, Photographic Archive)

Barley Soup

3	tablespoons butter	2	teaspoons salt
1	cup chopped green onions	¼	teaspoon black pepper
8	cups beef broth	1	bay leaf
¾	cup barley	1	35-ounce can tomatoes with
2	teaspoons ground cumin		juice, crushed or mashed
1½	teaspoons chili powder	3	tablespoons chopped parsley
¾	teaspoon dried thyme		

Heat butter over moderately high heat. Add the onions and cook until softened and lightly browned, about 8 minutes. Stir in 8 cups beef broth, the barley, cumin, chili powder, thyme, salt, pepper, and bay leaf and bring to a boil. Add the tomatoes and their juice. Reduce the heat to moderately low and simmer, partially covered, about 1½ hours. Remove bay leaf, sprinkle with parsley, and serve. Serves 8 to 10.

Rachel's Macaroni and Cheese

2½	cups elbow macaroni	2¼	cups milk
2	quarts boiling water	1	teaspoon salt
½	cup butter		Dash of pepper
¼	cup flour	2	cups grated sharp Cheddar cheese

Preheat oven to 350°. Cook macaroni in boiling water until tender. Drain. Melt butter in saucepan. Stir in flour until smooth. Add milk gradually. Cook, stirring constantly until sauce bubbles. Season with salt and pepper. In a casserole dish alternate layers of macaroni and cheese. Pour the hot sauce over the top and sprinkle with remaining cheese. Bake for 35 minutes or until golden brown. Serves 6.

Vegetable Soup with Hamburger

2 pounds hamburger	2 cups chopped cabbage
½ cup barley	2 cups sliced potatoes
1 cup chopped onion	2 to 3 cups tomato juice
1 cup chopped celery	Salt to taste
1 cup chopped carrots	

Place hamburger in large kettle, cover with water, and when water boils add barley. Reduce heat to simmer and cook until barley is almost done, 30 to 40 minutes. Add vegetables and cook, adding water as needed. Add tomato juice and salt last, just before serving. This makes a thick soup.

Tuna Loaf

1 8-ounce package cream cheese, softened	½ teaspoon Tabasco
2 tablespoons chili sauce	2 7-ounce cans white tuna, drained and flaked
2 tablespoons dried parsley	Parsley
1 teaspoon chopped onion	

Blend first 5 ingredients. Add tuna and mix well. Pack firmly in 4-cup serving bowl lined with plastic wrap. Chill 4 hours. Unmold onto a platter covered with chopped lettuce and serve with crackers. Decorate with parsley.

Baked Beans

1 29-ounce can pork and beans	1 tablespoon bacon grease
⅔ cup ketchup	1 can drained cubed pineapple
⅔ cup brown sugar	4 to 5 strips of bacon, fried crisp
½ cup chopped onion	

Mix pork and beans, ketchup, brown sugar, onion, and bacon grease. Bake in 350° oven for 30 minutes. Add cubed pineapple. Bake for 20 to 30 minutes in 350° to 400° oven. Put crisp bacon on top before serving.

Pork with Vegetables

4	pounds lean pork	4	carrots, diced
1	pound green peas	3	cups water
1	pound green beans	2	tablespoons butter
1	15-ounce can corn	2	teaspoons salt
1	15-ounce can tomatoes	1½	teaspoons ground pepper

Cut pork into cubes, brown in shortening in a large Dutch oven. Add other ingredients. Simmer until thick, about 2½ hours.

SIDE DISHES

Shrimp Dip

1	16-ounce jar Cheese Whiz	½	cup chopped green onion
2	8-ounce packages cream cheese	4	½-ounce cans drained shrimp
1	cup chopped celery		

Whip cheeses together with mixer and add remaining ingredients.

Ham Balls

1	pound ham, ground	½	cup cider vinegar
1½	pounds fresh pork, ground	1½	cups brown sugar
2	eggs, well beaten	½	cup water
1	cup milk	1	teaspoon mustard
2	cups breadcrumbs		

Make first 5 ingredients into balls. Mix remaining ingredients, pour over ham balls, and bake in covered skillet for 1½ hours at 325°. Turn after half the baking time.

Ham and Cheese on Bun

Spread:
- 1 stick soft butter
- 2 tablespoons poppy seeds
- 2 tablespoons minced onion
- 1 tablespoon prepared mustard
- 2 drops Worcestershire sauce

Sandwiches:
- Ham slices
- Swiss cheese slices
- Hamburger buns

Mix spread ingredients until smooth. Place ham slices and Swiss cheese on hamburger buns generously covered with spread. Wrap each bun in foil. Heat in oven at 350° for 20 minutes or until very hot.

Green Garden Salad

- Pepper
- Salt
- ½ cup sugar
- ½ cup cider vinegar
- 2 or 3 carrots, chopped
- 1 small head cabbage, shredded
- 2 chopped green peppers
- 1 chopped onion
- 2 cooked, chopped medium new potatoes, unpeeled
- 3 or 4 radishes, sliced

Mix pepper, salt, sugar, and vinegar. Mix other ingredients together with vinegar mixture and serve with radish on top.

Baked Grits

- 1 cup raw grits
- 3 cups boiling water
- 1½ teaspoons salt
- 3 tablespoons butter
- 1 teaspoon black pepper
- 1 small green bell pepper, chopped
- 6 slices bacon, cooked and crumbled
- 1 medium onion, chopped
- 2 eggs, slightly beaten
- 1 cup milk

Cook grits in boiling water that salt has been added to. Cook until thick, about 15 minutes. Add butter, pepper, green pepper, bacon, onions. Then add eggs and milk. Mix well. Pour into a buttered baking dish. Bake about 45 minutes at 375°.

Fried Peaches

. . . .

4   *freestone peaches*   8   *teaspoons sugar*
2   *tablespoons butter or margarine*

Wash and dry peaches. Do not peel. Cut in half lengthwise and remove stones. Melt butter in skillet over medium heat. Add peaches and cook until brown around edges, turning occasionally. Turn peaches cup-side up and place 1 teaspoon of sugar in each peach hollow. Cover and reduce to lowest heat. Cook 20 to 25 minutes. Remove cover and cook a few minutes to reduce juice. Remove peaches to serving bowl, turn up heat, and cook juice a few more minutes to thicken. Spoon over peaches.

Note: Use only freestone peaches. Increase the recipe by allowing 1 peach per person and 1 teaspoon of sugar to each hollow.

In October 1996 Dolly was working in one part of Dollywood, her amusement park in Pigeon Forge, Randy was performing in another part of the park, and I was signing copies of my book. I don't think any of us knew the others were there until someone got me and Dolly together. (Courtesy of Curtis W. Hilbun)

We had cherry and plum trees in our front yard, where we lived at Locust Ridge (Dolly's Tennessee Mountain Home). I think our Great Grandpa, Jim Owens, planted part or most of the fruit trees and berry bushes on the place.

He and Great Grandma Lindy had owned this property when they first moved to this part of Tennessee from North Carolina. I remember how beautiful the trees were in the spring when they bloomed, and bees, birds, and butterflies were everywhere. Later, we would cover the cherry trees with canvas (cheesecloth), the same kind we put over the tobacco beds in the spring. This was to keep the birds from getting all the cherries, but they still got their part!

Fried Zucchini

4 small zucchini	Dash onion powder
1 cup cornmeal	Vegetable oil
1 teaspoon salt	Parmesan cheese (optional)
½ teaspoon pepper	

Slice zucchini ½ inch thick. Mix other ingredients together (except oil). Dip zucchini in cornmeal mixture until coated. Fry in vegetable oil. Garnish with Parmesan cheese if desired. Same recipe may be used for green tomatoes, okra, and eggplant (peel eggplant).

Fried Eggplant

1 eggplant	Flour
1 egg	3 ripe tomatoes
½ teaspoon salt	Vegetable oil

Peel and slice the eggplant. Beat the egg and add salt. Dip the eggplant slices into egg and then into flour. Fry in hot fat until tender and cooked through. Cut tomato into thick slices. Dip in flour. Brown until tender in a greased pan. Serve hot, placing the fried tomato on the fried eggplant. Serves 6.

Creamed New Potatoes

....

6 small new potatoes
½ cup cream
1 tablespoon butter
1 teaspoon lemon juice

Salt and pepper
Parsley
Caraway seeds

Scrape the new potatoes and let stand for 30 minutes in cold water. Boil in salted water until tender. Put them in a saucepan with the cream, butter, lemon juice, and seasoning. Shake well over heat. Sprinkle with chopped parsley and caraway seeds.

Sinful Potatoes

....

2 pounds hash browns
1 cup Cheddar cheese, shredded
½ onion, chopped
1 10¾-ounce can cream of chicken soup

1 stick butter or margarine, melted
1 pint sour cream
Salt and pepper

Mix well, bake about 45 minutes at 350°.

Hot Potato Salad

....

4 medium potatoes
1 small onion
½ stick butter
1 tablespoon flour
1 tablespoon cider vinegar

½ teaspoon salt
½ teaspoon pepper
½ teaspoon onion seasoning
¼ teaspoon paprika

Cook potatoes with skins. Cook onion in water with salt (cook quite dry). When cool, add butter blended with flour. Add vinegar, enough water to cover potatoes, salt, and seasoning (except for paprika). Heat, pour over potatoes that have been peeled and sliced, and add a little butter. Put in buttered baking dish, sprinkle top with paprika, and place in 200° oven for 1 hour.

Randy, Rachel, and Floyd like singing at any family gathering.

Best Green Beans Ever!

. . . .

32 ounces frozen green beans	¼ cup Louisiana Hot Sauce
1½ cups water	1 to 2 slices bacon
1½ tablespoons garlic powder	

Empty frozen green beans into a 2-quart saucepan. Add water, garlic powder, and hot sauce; lift up beans to mix ingredients. Cut bacon strips into 4 pieces each. Turn burner to medium-high until liquid begins to boil; turn heat to simmer and cook at least an hour. Serves 4 to 6.

BREADS

Tomato Fritters

. . . .

2 cups green, ripe, or half and half   1 cup cornmeal
   tomatoes, chopped   ½ teaspoon salt

Mix ingredients into tomatoes and fry in a hot pan of grease or oil. For a different dish, substitute flour for meal, add 1 teaspoon pepper, and fry the same way. Both versions are very good. Makes 8 fritters.

Terrific Biscuits

. . . .

2 cups self-rising flour   2 tablespoons sugar
1 cup milk   4 tablespoons mayonnaise

Put all in mixing bowl. Mix with wire whisk until all is moistened. Do not over-beat. Divide batter equally between 10 greased muffin tins. Bake at 350° for 25 to 30 minutes until brown. Let cool 5 minutes before serving.

Spoon Bread

. . . .

1 cup yellow cornmeal   4 medium eggs, well beaten
2 cups boiling water   1 cup whole milk
4 tablespoons butter   Extra butter
1 teaspoon salt

Slowly add cornmeal to boiling water, stirring constantly until smooth. It will be thick. Add butter and salt. Cool until just warm. Then add eggs and milk. Beat for 2 or 3 minutes. Pour into greased casserole dish and bake at 375° for 35 minutes or until brown. Spoon onto serving plates while hot. Serve extra butter. Yields 10 to 12 servings.

DESSERTS AND SWEETS

Wild Pie

4   eggs, slightly beaten
½   cup margarine, melted
½   cup flour
2   cups milk

1   cup sugar
1   cup coconut
2   teaspoons vanilla extract

Mix all ingredients thoroughly. Pour into greased 10-inch pie plate. Bake at 350° for 1 hour or until center tests firm. Flour settles to form a crust. Serve with fresh berries and whipped cream.

When we had family picnics all the children usually had to get together for a picture. Front row (left to right): *Dwight Puckett, Bobby, Denver, Dolly, myself, and Randy.* Back row (left to right): *Dale Puckett, Cassie, Donna Puckett, Stella, and David. The Pucketts were the children of Dorothy Jo, my mother's youngest sister.*

Strawberry Fritters

Sift together ½ cup flour, ½ teaspoon baking powder, ⅛ teaspoon salt. Add 1 egg beaten very lightly, 2 tablespoons of milk, and 5 teaspoons melted butter. Drop 12 to 14 sliced strawberries in batter, coat well, and using a large spoon, drop into hot fat. Fry until lightly browned; drain on paper towels. Serve with sugar.

Fried Apple or Peach Pies

Filling:

2	tablespoons butter	½	teaspoon salt
3	cups peaches or apples (may be mixed), chopped	¼	teaspoon nutmeg
		¼	teaspoon cinnamon
1	cup sugar	1	teaspoon cornstarch

Melt butter, add all ingredients, and cook on medium heat until thick and fruit is tender.

Pastry:

3	cups flour	½	cup shortening
1½	teaspoons salt	¾	cup milk
2	teaspoons baking powder		

Combine flour, salt, and baking powder, cut in shortening until mixture is coarse like meal. Sprinkle milk gradually over flour mixture. Mix just until mixture forms a ball.

Divide pastry into 12 balls, roll each ball to about ¼-inch thickness. Cut into 6-inch circles. Place about 2 heaping tablespoons of fruit mixture on half of the circle. Fold top over. Dip fingers in a bowl of water and press top and bottom crust together using a fork dipped in flour to seal pastry edges firmly together. Fry pies in 1½ inches of shortening in a large skillet until golden brown. Yields about 12 pies.

Blackberry or Cherry Cobbler

Filling:

1	cup sugar	1	tablespoon cornstarch
1	cup water	3	cups fresh blackberries or cherries
½	stick butter	1	tablespoon cinnamon

Heat ingredients in 2-quart saucepan until bubbly. Mash part of blackberries or pitted cherries in the sauce, leaving most of them whole. Set aside while preparing crust.

Crust:

1	cup all-purpose flour	1	tablespoon baking powder
½	teaspoon salt	3	tablespoons shortening
½	cup milk	¼	teaspoon cinnamon
¼	cup sugar		

Blend ingredients in mixing bowl until fairly thick. Pour blackberry or cherry sauce in baking dish that is 2 inches high. Drop tablespoons of dough in lumps on top of hot blackberry or cherry sauce. Bake at 350° until dough is done and brown.

Waffles with Maple Syrup

2	cups flour	3	eggs, separated
2	teaspoons baking powder	1½	cups milk
2½	teaspoons sugar	6	tablespoons butter
½	teaspoon salt		

Sift flour and measure, then sift flour, baking powder, sugar, and salt, 3 times. To the well-beaten egg yolks, add flour alternately with milk. Add butter which has been melted over hot water and cooled. Fold in stiffly beaten egg whites. For cheese waffles, add ½ to ¾ cup grated cheese to above batter. Bake in hot waffle iron. Serve with homemade maple syrup (see recipe on next page).

Maple Syrup

3½ cups brown sugar
2 cups boiling water

1 teaspoon maple flavoring

Pour brown sugar into boiling water. Add maple flavoring. Stir well, allow to stand 24 hours to blend before using. This makes 1 quart of maple syrup.

Sweet Potato Pudding

Grate 4 good-size sweet potatoes, add 1 pint milk, 2 eggs beaten light, 2 cups sugar, ¼ teaspoon nutmeg. Bake in 325° oven ½ hour. Before removing from oven, top with marshmallows and brown sugar. Serve hot or cold with whipped cream.

Fruit Cobbler

2 cups flour
¾ teaspoon salt
2 teaspoons baking powder
4 tablespoons butter
1 scant cup milk

4 cups fruit or 2 16-ounce cans of peaches, apples, or berries
Sugar
Nutmeg

Sift flour, salt, and baking powder together and mix. Work butter into mixture, add milk. Roll on bread board about ¼ inch thick. In buttered pudding dish place sliced ripe peaches (or other fruit), sprinkle with sugar, nutmeg, pieces of butter, 1 tablespoon flour. Cover with dough, bake in 350° oven for 30 minutes. Serve with cream.

Laura Parton (left) and Lona Parton, aunts of my father, got their picture taken with Dolly at the Robert F. Thomas Chapel in Dollywood. The chapel was named after the doctor who delivered Dolly, David, Denver, and me.

Peach Cobbler

....

About 10 peaches, peeled, pitted, and sliced
1 teaspoon lemon juice

1 cup sugar
2 tablespoons butter
1 pie crust, unbaked

Place peaches in bottom of baking dish, sprinkle with lemon juice then sugar. Place dots of butter over the top of this. Cover the top with a pie crust. Prick with a fork, bake until brown about 30 minutes at 350°.

Rhubarb Custard Pie

3   cups rhubarb, chopped and
     cooked
1   cup sugar
2   tablespoons flour
¼   teaspoon cinnamon

¼   teaspoon salt
1   tablespoon butter, softened
2   eggs, slightly beaten
1   pie shell, unbaked

Combine ingredients and place in an unbaked pie shell. Bake at 400° for 10 minutes or 350° for 30 to 35 minutes.

My Favorite Chocolate Pie

3   cups sugar
8   tablespoons cocoa
¼   teaspoon salt
1   12-ounce can evaporated milk
2   cups water

8   egg yolks
8   tablespoons cornstarch
1   stick margarine
2   large or 3 medium pie shells,
     baked

Mix sugar, cocoa, salt. Add milk, water, and egg yolks. Add cornstarch. Cook until thick. Add margarine. Fill 2 large or 3 medium baked pie shells.

Meringue:
8   egg whites
⅓   cup powdered sugar

Dash cream of tartar

Beat egg whites until stiff. Add sugar and tartar. Cover pies with meringue. Bake at 375° for 5 to 10 minutes or just until brown.

Caramel Pudding

1 cup brown sugar	⅓ cup cornstarch
½ cup butter	¾ cup shredded coconut
2 cups hot milk	1 teaspoon vanilla

Melt sugar and butter over hot water, add hot milk. Blend in cornstarch, which has been dissolved in a little milk. Cook in double boiler until thick. Remove from heat. Cool. Add shredded coconut and vanilla.

Julia's Applesauce Black Walnut Cake

1¾ cup sifted flour	1 teaspoon baking soda
1 cup black walnuts	¼ teaspoon salt
1 cup raisins	1 teaspoon cinnamon
½ cup butter	½ teaspoon cloves
1 cup sugar	1 cup thick, sweetened applesauce
1 egg	

Sift a little flour over the walnuts and raisins. Cream butter with sugar and beat in egg. Add walnuts and raisins. In a separate bowl, sift flour, baking soda, salt, and spices. Stir flour mixture into first mixture. Add applesauce that has been heated. Bake in 9-inch tube pan in 350° oven for 1 hour. Best with vanilla or white butter frosting.

Orange Cake

1½ cups sugar
¾ cup butter
3 eggs
1 cup cold water

Rind of 1 orange, grated
2 cups flour
3 teaspoons baking powder

Cream sugar and butter. Add eggs one at a time. Beating well, add water, orange rind, flour, and baking powder. Mix well and bake at 350° for 45 minutes or until brown.

Chocolate Butterscotch Pie

3 tablespoons butter
1 cup brown sugar
1 cup milk
⅓ cup Jell-O chocolate pudding mix

1 teaspoon vanilla
2 eggs, separated
3 tablespoons sugar
1 pie crust, baked

Put butter and brown sugar in skillet and heat. Add milk, chocolate pudding dissolved in an additional ½ cup milk, and vanilla. Let boil about 3 minutes, beat in egg yolks. Pour into baked pie crust. Cover pie with meringue made of stiffly beaten whites of eggs and sugar. Place in oven at 375°; cook for length of time indicated on pudding package.

Baked Rhubarb

3 cups rhubarb
½ teaspoon salt
1 cup sugar

¼ teaspoon cinnamon
¼ teaspoon nutmeg (optional)

Remove rhubarb leaves. Do not peel. Wash stalks, cut in 1-inch pieces. Place in baking dish, stir salt and sugar into water, pour over rhubarb. Bake in 350° oven for 15 to 25 minutes or until tender. Add cinnamon or nutmeg if desired.

Never Fail Pie Crust

4 cups self-rising flour	1 egg, lightly beaten
1 tablespoon sugar	½ cup cold water
½ tablespoon salt	1 tablespoon cider vinegar
1½ cups shortening	

Mix flour, sugar, and salt with shortening. Add egg, water, and vinegar gradually to other ingredients. Mix flour until moistened well. Roll out on floured board. Makes 4 pie crusts. Prick with a fork and bake in a 425° oven for 12 to 15 minutes.

All of us played music. Grandpa Walter Parton, my father's father, played the banjo and taught Papa to play too.

Blackberry Pie

Pastry:

- 2 cups flour
- Pinch salt
- ¼ cup shortening
- 1 tablespoon sugar
- 2 tablespoons cold water

Sift the flour and salt in a mixing bowl, cut shortening into small pieces and rub into the flour with fingers until the mixture resembles fine breadcrumbs. Stir in sugar and enough water to draw the mixture together. Transfer to a lightly floured board and knead the dough briefly until smooth. Wrap in aluminum foil and chill for at least 30 minutes. Divide the dough in 2 parts and roll out on floured board to a circle large enough to fit the base of an 8-inch pan. Chill in refrigerator for about 15 minutes.

Filling:

- ½ pound blackberries
- 1 pound tart or cooking apples
- ½ lemon, juice and finely grated rind
- ½ cup sugar
- 2 tablespoons flour

Put washed blackberries in mixing bowl. Peel, core, and slice apples. Fold into the blackberries with lemon rind and juice, then add sugar (amount needed will depend on tartness of apples) and flour. Spoon the fruit mixture into pie pastry. Roll out the remaining dough to a circle for a top. Lay it over the filling, pressing down and sealing the edges with water. Flute the edges with your fingers or crimp with prongs of a fork. Bake covered with foil at 350° for 40 to 50 minutes or until a toothpick inserted into top of the pie pierces tender apples. Remove the foil from the pie for 10 to 15 minutes of cooking to crisp up the pastry. To serve, sprinkle with a mixture of white and brown sugar and leave to rest for 5 to 10 minutes. May also serve with ice cream.

Doughnuts

1 cake Fleischmann's yeast
1 tablespoon sugar
¼ cup milk, scalded
1½ cups sifted flour
½ cup sugar

3 tablespoons butter
¼ teaspoon mace or cinnamon
1 egg
  Vegetable oil

Dissolve yeast and 1 tablespoon sugar in lukewarm milk. Add 1½ cups flour and beat well. Cover and let rise for about 1 hour. Add rest of ingredients. Knead lightly. Place in greased bowl and let rise ½ hour. Turn on floured board. Roll and cut. Let rise 45 minutes. Fry in deep fat. Drain on paper towels and roll in sugar before serving.

Dutch Apple Pie

6 Granny Smith apples, peeled, cored, and sliced
¾ cup white sugar
¼ cup brown sugar

1 tablespoon flour
1 teaspoon lemon juice
¼ teaspoon salt
½ cup sour cream

Mix apples with remaining ingredients. Sprinkle with cinnamon and ¼ teaspoon nutmeg. Top with topping of ½ cup butter, ½ cup flour, and ½ cup brown sugar. Bake in a greased pie pan at 375° for 40 minutes to 1 hour.

Note: If you don't use sour cream then double the flour in the filling ingredients.

Fruit Ice

3 ripe bananas
3 oranges, juiced
3 lemons, juiced
2 cups sugar

⅓ cup pineapple juice
3 cups water
  Pinch salt

Rub bananas through sieve. Add fruit juices, sugar, water, and salt. Blend well and freeze.

Every year, usually in September, we have a Parton and Owens family reunion.

Thumbprint Cookies

½ cup butter	2 teaspoons baking powder
⅔ cup sugar	1 egg white, beaten
2 eggs	¾ cup chopped walnuts
1 teaspoon vanilla	Jelly
2½ cups flour	

In bowl cream butter and sugar. Beat in eggs and vanilla, add flour and baking powder. Chill at least 3 hours. Roll dough in balls, dip in egg white and nuts. Bake at 350° for 10 minutes. Make depression, fill with jelly. Bake 5 more minutes.

Variation: Malted Milk Balls

1 recipe basic dough, 60 malted milk balls, 2 cups flaked coconut. Roll 1 teaspoon of dough around a milk ball. Roll in coconut. Bake at 350° for 12 minutes. Makes 5 dozen.

My mother's side of the family at a birthday party for her father, Grandpa Jake. Front row (left to right): Aunt Dorothy Jo, Uncle Bill, Cousin Tina. Back row (left to right): Aunt Estelle, Grandpa Jake, my mother, and Tammy Owens.

Fruit Cocktail Cake

1 cup sugar	2 teaspoons baking soda
2 eggs, lightly beaten	1 cup chopped pecans (or other
14 ounces fruit cocktail	nuts)
2 cups self-rising flour	½ cup brown sugar

Stir together sugar, eggs, and fruit cocktail. Sift flour and baking soda together and stir in other mixture. Put in 8x12-inch greased pan. Mix together chopped pecans and brown sugar. Sprinkle on top of cake and bake at 300° for 35 minutes.

Icing:

1 cup margarine	1 cup coconut
1 cup white sugar	1 teaspoon vanilla extract
5 ounces evaporated milk	½ cup chopped nuts

Combine ingredients, except for vanilla and nuts. Cook for 2 minutes on stove, add vanilla and nuts, and pour on cake as soon as the cake is removed from the oven, while it is still hot.

Cantaloupe Pie

1 cantaloupe (ripe)	½ teaspoon nutmeg
1 rounded teaspoon flour	½ stick margarine
½ cup sugar	1 pie shell, unbaked

Peel cantaloupe, remove seeds, and cut into small pieces. Place in unbaked pie shell. Sprinkle flour, sugar, and nutmeg over cantaloupe. Add margarine in small slices on top of this mixture. Top with crust and bake at 350° for 15 minutes. Reduce heat to 300° and bake 30 minutes longer or until browned.

Making cider in Giles County, Tennessee. (Courtesy of Tennessee State Library and Archives)

Canning, Preserving, and Special Treats

O f course, I grew up when we couldn't run out to the 7-Eleven for milk or coffee or other things that we consider "necessities" now. And, even if there had been such things then as those "convenience" stores, our family couldn't have gone to them anyway.

For most of the time when I was growing up, as I said, we lived off the land. So, making the best use of what we did have was pretty important.

And it wasn't just food that we used in a lot of ways. Mother and her mother and grandmother dried flowers and made potpourri. They called them sachets. I still make them occasionally with spices and flowers.

Coffee was not an everyday thing. We often used a beverage—a coffee substitute—called Postum. The kids were allowed to drink it with sugar and milk, often at our grandparents' homes. Just the other day, I bought a jar, and my sisters and nieces had some—almost just like we used to. It was a special memory that I'm glad we could share with the "young'uns."

Back then "oleo" didn't look like it looks now. Sometimes we got it with a powder that was dark orange or red, and we had to mix it into the oleo to make it look like butter. I didn't know then that the dairy lobby got laws passed that prevented the people who made oleo from making it actually look like butter. We didn't care—it tasted pretty good to us.

We ate mulberries as they fell from the trees, and we gathered them for pies and preserves. When they got ripe, they all seemed to fall from the trees within a week, and they covered the ground. Sometimes we used them for feeding the hogs or the chickens. Nothing went to waste.

We pickled okra and peaches and pretty much anything we could think of. We made preserves from peaches, pears, huckleberries, and persimmons. As I mentioned, we had lots of different kinds of apples, and we used them for apple butter and jelly and cider.

Now, Papa liked to make the best use of some of the natural bounty of the land. He would occasionally make—and drink—a little wine and "brandy" and beer and maybe some "shine." I remember "peach brandy." It sounded elegant then. Mother thought it was a sin and that Papa was going straight to Hell. On the other hand, there's something to be said for the view that if God hadn't thought a little wine was okay then we wouldn't have any grapes. Of course, Papa never let us share in his natural beverages.

The kids used to pick honey locust beans off the trees near where we went to school. We would eat them while the fruit—the insides—was still green and firm. Mother used them to make a tea her grandmother had taught her to make. We would mash the beans into a pulp for her. She would pour hot water over the pulp and then strain it, adding some honey or sugar if we had it. We thought it was extra special because she called it "Indian tea." Some of Mother's people on one side are part Cherokee. She also made an "Indian pudding" from "possum grapes"—a wild grape. It is a delicious grape that always remains a little tart. Mother cooked the grapes down, then made a pudding from cornmeal and sugar, baked it into a custard, and served it hot.

My grandmother Rena Owens always planted a "late garden." Usually it was planted in the first week of June—later and the first frost might get the garden. These were the vegetables that we most often canned in order to have them throughout the winter.

Hogs were usually slaughtered in the fall to put up bacon—side meat—and hams for the winter. Very little of a hog went to waste. It was used for making soap. The cans we used for molasses and honey were called "lard cans" because at killing time the lard was rendered over an open fire and an iron kettle and then poured into the cans for storing. If we had no butter, we used the pork lard to make cookies and cakes. When we ran out of lard in the summer, Mother sometimes used fatback with the skin on to grease the bread pans. You could use it over and over again.

Anyway, we understood the true meaning of the term "preserves." We had to use all we had as best we could. We did.

SAUCES AND DRESSINGS

Butter Sauce

1 cup sugar
½ cup cream
3 tablespoons butter

1 cup light corn syrup
½ teaspoon vanilla or lemon extract

Blend all ingredients except extract. Cook in double boiler until smooth and thick. Add flavoring.

Butterscotch Sauce

1 cup brown sugar
3½ tablespoons butter
½ cup heavy cream

1 cup dark corn syrup
½ teaspoon vanilla

Put all ingredients (except vanilla) into double boiler and cook until smooth and thick. Remove from heat and add vanilla.

Fudge Sauce for Ice Cream or Cake

2 cups sugar
1 cup brown sugar
1 cup cocoa
3 tablespoons sifted flour

1½ cups water
¼ cup butter
1 teaspoon vanilla or almond extract

In a double boiler, mix together sugars, cocoa, flour, and water. Cook 8 to 10 minutes over hot water until quite thick. Stir constantly. Remove from heat and mix in butter and flavoring.

Hollandaise Sauce

. . . .

2	tablespoons butter	½	teaspoon salt
2	tablespoons flour		Few grains red pepper
½	cup hot milk or boiling water	2	egg yolks
¼	teaspoon white pepper	1	tablespoon lemon juice

In a double boiler, melt butter, blend in flour, stir well. Slowly add milk, seasonings, bring to boiling point. Cool. Add beaten egg yolks, slowly add lemon juice. Cook mixture in double boiler.

Medium White Sauce

. . . .

3	tablespoons butter	1	teaspoon salt
3	tablespoons flour	⅛	teaspoon pepper
2	cups milk		

Melt butter in saucepan and blend in flour. Stir in milk; bring to a boil, and add salt and pepper. Cook for about 7 minutes over low heat, stirring frequently.

Thin White Sauce

. . . .

Follow Medium White Sauce recipe, but use 1 less tablespoon of both butter and flour.

Thick White Sauce

. . . .

Follow Medium White Sauce recipe, but reduce heat and cook 15 minutes, stirring occasionally, adding 1 tablespoon more of butter and 1 tablespoon more of flour.

Cheese Sauce

Follow recipe for Medium White Sauce, and melt 1 cup of grated or diced cheese into the sauce.

Hot Dog Sauce

2 small cans tomato paste	1 pound ground beef, browned
1 small can tomato sauce	2 cups water
2 large onions, diced	½ teaspoon garlic powder
2 tablespoons oil	Salt and cumin to taste
1 tablespoon chili powder	

Mix, simmer until thick.

Papa has a secret recipe for making kraut, which he is making here for canning while I watch. It is so special and so secret, he would not let me put the recipe in this book.

Cucumber Sauce

½ cup cream
½ teaspoon salt
Pinch of black pepper
2 tablespoons cider vinegar

2 small cucumbers, peeled,
chopped, and drained
Paprika

Beat cream to thick consistency. Add salt, pepper, and vinegar, stir. Add 2 cucumbers. Add paprika to taste.

Tartar Sauce

1½ tablespoons minced sour pickle
Paprika
1 teaspoon minced capers
1 tablespoon minced chives

1 teaspoon minced green olives
Few drops onion juice
1 tablespoon vinegar
1 cup mayonnaise

Mix all thoroughly. Ready to use. Use celery salt, onion seasoning, and red pepper if desired.

Meat Sauce

1 cup tomato sauce
1 tablespoon chili sauce
¾ tablespoon lemon juice
¼ teaspoon ground red pepper

1 teaspoon grated horseradish
¼ teaspoon celery salt
½ teaspoon onion seasoning

Mix and chill.

Meatless Spaghetti Sauce

4 tablespoons olive oil
1 medium onion, minced
1 clove garlic, chopped
1 cup celery, diced
1 teaspoon salt
¼ teaspoon pepper
1 tablespoon molasses
1 quart tomato juice
1 12-ounce box spaghetti, cooked

Heat oil in Dutch oven (or chicken fryer). Add onion and garlic and sauté until light brown. Add remaining ingredients and cook over low heat 30 minutes. Serve over cooked spaghetti. Serves 6 to 8.

In the early seventies I wrote an article for *Dolly's Fan Club Journal* and also put the story in my book *In The Shadow of a Song* in the early eighties. The article was about a family of skunks that lived near our barn. Several people have liked it enough to use it in books about our family. Here is my original version:

One day our Uncle Alden Owens (Mother's baby brother), my brothers David and Denver, and I lay in wait for these cute baby skunks. We were always catching baby squirrels, rabbits, and birds, but we had never had a baby skunk to play with. We got them! But, the mother didn't take kindly to kidnappers and her aim was good. When Mother found out she made us turn them loose. She washed us in gallons of tomato juice and burned our clothes. Until then, we had only used tomato juice for food, never to take a bath in. Our hearts were broken. We waited on the side of the road for Papa to tell him our awful troubles. He often took our part about the way Mother handled our tragedies.

So, it's always good to be prepared. We never knew how many cans of anything we might need or what it might be used for! Mother and Papa just filled every can!

Horseradish Sauce

2 tablespoons grated or finely
   chopped onions
2 tablespoons butter (not
   margarine)

2 tablespoons flour
2 cups light cream or half-and-half
6 tablespoons prepared horseradish

Sauté onions in butter until lightly brown, add flour, and mix well. Slowly add cream, stirring constantly. Add horseradish and beat thoroughly. Great for roast beef, corned beef, etc. Yields 10 to 12 servings.

Aunt Cora was my father's aunt and enjoyed canning.

Chutney Salad Dressing

¼ teaspoon salt	4 tablespoons olive oil
¼ teaspoon paprika	1 teaspoon grated hard cheese
1½ teaspoons sugar	1 tablespoon lemon juice
2 tablespoons chutney	

Blend all ingredients, mix well before using.

SPREADABLES

Molasses and Butter Spread

(For hot biscuits and corn cakes)

1 cup molasses	1 pound butter, softened

Blend molasses and butter thoroughly and chill.

We grew cane for molasses. In the fall, we had several large metal cans for molasses. Papa also kept honey bees and we used the cans for honey as well. We called the cans simply "lard cans." In the winter at hog killing time, when the lard was rendered over an open fire in the iron kettle, it would then be stored in the cans.

Papa sold molasses, honey, lard, sugar, and salt-cured hams and shoulders to supplement our income. He also sold tobacco. We picked and sold beans and tomatoes by the bushel.

Papa says he raised cane and kids. We used lots of honey and molasses to cook with.

Apple Butter

(This slices.)

2 cups tart apples, peeled and finely
   chopped

2 cups sugar
½ teaspoon cinnamon

Combine ingredients. Cook until mixture is boiling. Then it will start getting thick and slide from spoon. When it does this, it is done.

Our mother used to pack our lunches in brown paper bags. I don't remember owning a lunch box, but our Papa had a large black lunch box with a red and gray thermos bottle.

Mother remembers taking a small lard bucket to school with her lunch inside it—milk in a glass jar with a lid and a potato (maybe) or beans and corn bread. Her favorite was a biscuit with white or brown sugar and butter or a slice of apple butter on a biscuit.

We used to take ham and biscuits, fried potato biscuits, or peanut butter and jelly biscuits. We would trade our nice lunches off for store-bought bread with mayonnaise or salad dressing only. I think we were ashamed of our homemade lunches and thought the white breads and spreads were fancy. They were treats, for the older ones of us, because we didn't have that at home at that time.

We called loaf bread "light bread." Sometimes even now we will say to someone going to the store, "Don't forget a loaf of light bread!"

JAMS, JELLIES, AND PRESERVES

Boiling Water Bath for Jams, Jellies, and Preserves

PLACE hot filled jars in hot pack canner in hot water, add additional water to cover top of jars. Place lid on water bath container and bring to a quick rolling boil. Start processing time then and not before water returns to boiling. Adjust heat to maintain a steady boil. When time is completed, carefully raise lid away from body to allow steam to escape and prevent burns. Immediately remove jars from canner. Let jars cool naturally (avoid drafts) on a rack. Do not cover. When jars are at room temperature, label with name of product and date. Store canned foods in a cool dry place.

Jelly and preserves should be in the boiling water bath for 5 to 6 minutes, jams for 8 to 10 minutes. Relish, pickles, and chow-chow should be in the bath for 10 to 15 minutes.

Raspberry, Strawberry, Blackberry, or Gooseberry Jelly

1   quart berries
1   cup water

1   envelope fruit pectin
3   level cups sugar

Wash and stem berries, crush thoroughly. Scald, using 1 cup water. Turn into cheesecloth bag, drain juice into bowl. Add sufficient water to give 2 cups of juice. Put fruit juice in large pan or kettle, place on high heat. Gradually add fruit pectin, bring to boil, and stir carefully to prevent any lumps. After pectin is thoroughly dissolved, add sugar. As soon as mixture is boiling vigorously, start timing and allow to boil thoroughly 2 minutes. Stir continuously while boiling. Skim off top, pour immediately into hot sterilized jars, seal, and place in hot bath.

In the mountains where we lived, watermelons were small but sweet. Cantaloupes did better. Sometimes people would have watermelons, cantaloupes, and peaches to sell from the beds of pick-up trucks. We had to have some. We used them for pies, relish, and punch. We gathered blueberries, gooseberries, and huckleberries by the gallons.

Gooseberry Jam

5   pounds gooseberries
4   ounces orange juice
1   box seedless raisins (white raisins
     may be used)

5   pounds sugar

Partially cook gooseberries, orange juice, and raisins, then add sugar. Cook until right consistency for jam. Pour into hot sterilized jars, seal, and place in hot bath.

Gooseberry, Blackberry, or Raspberry Jam

Clean fruit and mash in saucepan. Heat gradually to boiling point and add an equal quantity of sugar. Boil until thick, 4 or 5 minutes. Pour into hot sterilized jars, seal, and place in hot bath.

Old-fashioned Pumpkin or Sweet Potato Butter

2   cups cooked, well-drained fresh
     pumpkin or canned pumpkin, or
     2 cups cooked, mashed sweet
     potatoes

1   cup molasses
¼   teaspoon cinnamon
¼   teaspoon allspice

Combine all ingredients and cook well, stirring all the time, until thick. Place in hot sterilized jars, seal, and put in hot bath.

Wild Rose Jelly

1   quart spring water or distilled water
¼   cup rose petals, washed
1   pound sugar

Bring water to boiling, pour over rose petals. Add sugar, boil until clear. Pour through fine cloth or cheesecloth. Reheat. Pour into hot sterilized jars, seal, and place in hot bath.

Jelly or Syrup Made from Violets

1   quart spring water or distilled water
¼   cup fresh violet petals, washed
1   pound sugar

Bring water to a boil, pour over violet petals, mash into a paste. Keep adding water, add sugar. Boil until clear, strain through cheesecloth folded four times. Pour into hot sterilized jars, seal, and place in hot bath.

My grandmothers and my mother used to make cookies and candy with rose petals on top for decoration. Our mother always got carried away being creative. When she frosted a cake, she might just put mint leaves or flower petals on top, but only the kinds we could eat.

Blackberry Jelly

7   cups blackberries
7½   cups sugar
1   small box fruit pectin

Crush berries thoroughly, place in cheesecloth bag, squeeze out 4 cups of juice. Add sugar to juice and mix well, bring to boil over high heat. Add fruit pectin. Then bring to full boil for ½ minute. Remove from heat and skim. Pour into hot sterilized jars, seal, and place in hot bath.

Rhubarb Preserves

2 pounds rhubarb, cut in small
   pieces
   Juice of 1 lemon
1 cup finely chopped walnuts

4 cups sugar
4 teaspoons cooking wine
½ cup water

Place rhubarb in kettle. Add remaining ingredients. Boil for 1 hour, stirring often. When thick, pour into hot sterilized jars, seal, and place in hot bath.

Tomato Butter Preserves

About 24 ripe tomatoes (red or
yellow) peeled and mashed
1 cup water
1 tablespoon powdered mustard
1 cup brown sugar

1 cup white sugar
Juice from 2 lemons and the rind
grated extra fine (just the yellow
part)

Put tomatoes in the water and boil to the consistency of sauce. Put in mustard, sugars, lemon juice, and lemon rind. Cook 1 hour or until very thick. Put into hot sterilized jars, seal, and place in hot bath.

Blackberry Jam

3 cups crushed blackberries

3 cups sugar

Pick over berries carefully, wash, crush, and bring berries to hard boil. Boil 2 minutes, add sugar, stir until dissolved. Let boil 1 minute, put over low heat, beat hard 4 to 5 minutes with rotary or flat wire beater. The jam thickens with beating. Pour into hot sterilized jars, seal, and place in hot bath.

BEVERAGES

Spiced Tea

2	cups Tang	1	envelope lemonade Kool-Aid
2	cups sugar	1½	teaspoons ground cinnamon
1	cup instant unsweetened tea	¾	teaspoon ground cloves

Mix all ingredients together, store in jar with lid. To make tea, use 2 heaping teaspoons for each cup of water.

Hot Punch

2	quarts apple cider	2	cups orange juice
3	tablespoons red hot candies	2	cups pineapple juice
¼	teaspoon cinnamon		

Simmer ingredients about 20 minutes. Allow to settle. Serve hot with cinnamon sticks.

Raspberry Punch

½	cup sugar	2	3-ounce packages raspberry
4	cups water		Jell-O, dissolved in hot water
1	small can frozen lemonade	2	large cans pineapple juice
	concentrate	2	quarts ginger ale

Mix all ingredients and serve chilled.

Harvest Punch 1

. . . .

(My nephew, Bryan, calls this witches' brew.)

1 gallon apple juice or cider	1 handful red hot cinnamon candies
13 whole cloves (if you have the nerve), I use 11	1 2-liter bottle ginger ale
7 whole allspice	
1 12-ounce can frozen orange juice concentrate	

Combine ingredients and refrigerate overnight. Strain before serving. When ready to serve add ginger ale. This is good hot or cold.

Harvest Punch 2

. . . .

1 3-ounce package orange Jell-O	1 3-ounce package peach Jell-O
1 3-ounce package pineapple Jell-O	1 extra cup water

Use full amount of water in directions but use all hot water and no cold. Add an additional cup of water. Serve hot with cinnamon sticks.

My Watermelon Punch

. . . .

(From Stella's cookbook *Really Cooking*)

1 watermelon	1 teaspoon red food coloring
1 cup distilled water	1 quart ginger ale
2 cups sugar	

Cut watermelon in half. Scoop out contents, mash, and strain off watermelon juice, which should amount to about a gallon. Bring to a boil with distilled water and sugar till dissolved. Add food coloring and mix together well, then chill. When ready to serve, add ginger ale.

Regular Tea

1 cup sugar   7 regular tea bags
½ gallon hot water

Pour sugar into ½-gallon container and dissolve in hot water. Place tea bags in a pot of water and bring to a boil over medium heat. Jiggle tea bags up and down several times to get all the strength out of them. Discard tea bags and pour tea into container with sugar-water mixture. Fill remainder of container with cold water. Chill.

I took this picture of a kettle of hot sassafras tea at John Rice Irwin's Museum of Appalachia in Norris, Tennessee. Mother and my brother David used to make good sassafras tea, although not in a kettle like this. Ours was a round-bottomed kettle with short legs.

Cocoa Malted Milk

....

1 tablespoon cocoa	2 cups cream
1 tablespoon sugar	1 teaspoon vanilla
1 tablespoon malted milk	

Mix cocoa, sugar, and malted milk, add to a little cream that has been heated in double boiler. Cool then chill, add remaining cream and vanilla. Shake.

Hot Chocolate

....

3 tablespoons cocoa	Pinch of salt
2 tablespoons sugar	½ teaspoon vanilla
1 cup boiling water	Heavy cream, whipped
2 cups hot milk	

Mix cocoa and sugar with boiling water. Let boil 3 to 5 minutes. Add heated milk and salt. Flavor with a little vanilla. Serve with whipped cream.

Poor Man's Coffee

....

Mix well 2 quarts of wheat bran or wheat germ with 1 pint of yellow cornmeal. Add 4 well-beaten eggs and 1 cup of molasses.

Spread into a pan and put in oven to dry at 200°. Stir often while it is browning. 2 tablespoons makes enough for 4 cups. (My grandmother used 2 handfuls.) Strain before serving.

My grandmother used to make a substitute coffee that we children were allowed to drink. We added cream off the top of the milk. I remember it tasted something like malted milk.

5

Hunting Season

Someone once said the reason we have wild animals is so no one will ever starve. Maybe that's true, because it seems wild animals are hardly ever used for food anymore. I know my Papa hasn't hunted squirrel in a long, long time. He was never a big hunter anyway. Most of our wild meat came via neighbors, friends, and relatives that did hunt.

My Great-Uncle Phillip Owens used to hunt a lot, and when he came to visit, he came loaded with squirrel or rabbit meat. He and Papa would play the banjo, or he would just play for Papa because we wanted Papa to dance. Whoever wanted to would just join in. Mother was taught that dancing was a sin. We thought it was fun. So Mother cooked the meat into delicious recipes for us all to eat.

Many of these recipes are included for historical value only, but years ago our family used most of them at one time or another. I'm glad we did, because our parents kept us fed with some of these foods.

Even as late as 1956, some people in the South routinely hunted for their meat, especially the young men, who would have the macho symbol of a gray squirrel's tail on their car antenna. The cars were usually rusted from salt, as most of them came from "up North", as we called it—Chicago, Ohio, and Michigan. My brothers and sisters like to tease me about actually riding in one of those "up North" cars.

I remember I had the cutest boyfriend. His name was Clarence and his car was an old, 1939 Ford—hand-painted bright red and yellow over the rust. That car was so bad that if any of us had gotten a scratch from a door or a fender we would have had to get a tetanus shot to prevent lockjaw. I lost Clarence to a girl he thought was prettier and who liked his car better than I did.

I received a great letter from his youngest daughter this year. It reads, in part:

Dear Willadeene,

I'm a really big fan of yours. I started reading your books mainly because when you were a teenager, you dated my dad—you remember Clarence Stinnett? I read about it in your book *In the Shadow of a Song*. I liked what you wrote about him. I can't figure out what was wrong with him, breaking up with you, for what he thought was a prettier girl. I think you are beautiful. My favorite part in that book is when you tell about the rusty old car and the gray squirrel's tail. I am thirteen years old so you know how funny that is to me!

My daddy died when I was eleven years old. He had five children. I loved and miss my daddy so much.

Thank you for your time,
Melanie Stinnett

FISH AND GAME

Fried Squirrel or Rabbit

4	to 6 squirrels (or 2 rabbits), cut in serving pieces	3	eggs, beaten
2	teaspoons salt	1	cup milk
1½	teaspoons black pepper	2½	cups flour
			Vegetable oil

Marinate squirrel (or rabbit) overnight in mixture of salt, pepper, eggs, and milk. Remove from mixture and roll in flour. Fry for 15 to 20 minutes until golden brown.

Bear Roast

8	to 10 pounds bear meat (or beef)	2	cups flour
1	onion, quartered	2	teaspoons salt
1	hot red pepper	1	teaspoon black pepper

Boil meat for 2 hours in a large kettle with onion and hot red pepper. Then roll the meat in a mixture of the flour, salt, and black pepper and place in roasting pan with:

4	teaspoons butter	2	medium onions, quartered
1	cup celery, diced	1½	cups water
1	cup green bell pepper, sliced		

Bake at 350° for 2 hours or until tender. Add 8 medium potatoes, quartered, and cook 45 minutes more. Serves 10 to 12 people.

Rabbit Stew and Dumplings

4   rabbits
1   pound bacon, chopped and
    browned
1   large onion, chopped
6   quarts boiling water
1   16-ounce can stewed tomatoes
2   cups fresh corn, or 1 15½-ounce
    can cream-style corn
10 medium potatoes, quartered
1   teaspoon salt
1   teaspoon pepper
    Dash cayenne pepper
4   teaspoons sugar

Place rabbit, bacon, and onions in water, simmer for 2 hours. Remove rabbit and debone. Return rabbit to pot and add vegetables and seasonings. Simmer 1 hour. Drop dumplings on top and cook 10 to 15 minutes.

Dumplings:

2   cups sifted flour
3   teaspoons baking powder
1   teaspoon salt
3   teaspoons shortening
1   cup milk
    Black pepper, to taste

Mix all ingredients until coarse. Drop the dumplings into the stew with a teaspoon. Sprinkle top of dumplings with black pepper.

Groundhog

When groundhog is cleaned and cut in pieces be sure to remove the kernel from under the front legs to keep the meat from tasting strong. Salt and pepper. Roll in flour, put in hot fat, and fry until brown. Then put in pressure cooker with ½ inch water in bottom of cooker. Cook for 7 minutes with 15 pounds of pressure. Opossum can be cooked the same way with good results.

I remember when Dolly was a baby our Papa killed a couple of Mallard ducks on the river where we lived. Mother had thought they were so pretty and had said they would lay eggs and hatch off some baby ducks.

When Papa brought them into the kitchen, one cold winter afternoon, Mother was really angry with him. I guess they had given her a lot of pleasure as she watched them through the kitchen window. She asked Papa how he could have done such a thing—them being so pretty. He said, "So are the chickens and pigs. What's wrong with you anyway?" Since she wouldn't cook them, he did. And he was the only one who ate them.

They sure were surprised that I remembered that fight. They had forgotten it until I mentioned it, when I asked Papa how he cooked the ducks.

Papa's Special Duck

(No help from Mother)

2 ducks	2 teaspoons pepper
2 cups butter	2 apples, sliced
2 tablespoons flour	2 large potatoes, chopped
2 teaspoons salt	2 onions, chopped

Precook duck in simmering water 15 to 20 minutes, then drain. Let cool. Rub inside and outside with 1 cup of butter. Mix flour, salt, and pepper. Rub generously inside and outside with mixture.

Add apples, potatoes, and onions to cavity. Place duck, breast side up, in a baking pan. Baste with butter and bake at 350° for 3½ hours. Baste often with pan drippings. Serves four. A baked sweet potato or sweet chow-chow is good with this.

Papa's Drop Biscuits

1 cup flour	Milk to make a thick paste
¼ cup butter or shortening	

Combine ingredients. Drop in a well-greased pan with a tablespoon. Bake at 375° until brown—about 12 to 15 minutes.

Left to right: *Jack Boling, Wayne Parton, and Bufford Parton, cousins of my father, had their own picnic in the yard in the late 1940s.*

Roast Duck

2 mallards	½ cup margarine or butter, melted
1 medium potato, chopped	1 apple, chopped
2 carrots, sliced	1 large onion, chopped
1 teaspoon salt	Vegetable oil
1 teaspoon pepper	1½ cups boiling water

Preheat oven to 350°. Stuff duck with chopped potato and sliced carrots and precook in simmering water for 10 minutes. Remove and rub duck inside and out with salt and pepper and margarine. Add apples and onions to cavity. Place breast up on rack in shallow pan. Baste with vegetable oil. Add 1½ cups boiling water to pan. Place in oven for 3 to 4 hours. Baste often with pan drippings. Serves 4 to 6 people.

Duck Cooked in Sauce

. . . .

2 ducks	2 tablespoons pepper
2 quarts water	¾ cup margarine or butter, melted
1 tablespoon baking soda	½ cup lemon juice
2 tablespoons vinegar	1 tablespoon mustard
1 medium onion, chopped	1 cup celery, chopped
⅓ cup salt, plus 1 tablespoon	1 cup ketchup
1 medium potato, chopped	

Place ducks in large glass or plastic bowl with cover and marinate overnight in solution of water, soda, vinegar, onion, ⅓ cup salt, and potato. Marinate overnight. Preheat oven to 325°. Remove and rub inside and out with 1 tablespoon salt and 2 tablespoons pepper. Rub with margarine and sprinkle with flour. Place breast down on rack in roaster. To make sauce, mix lemon juice, mustard, celery, and ketchup. Heat mixture and pour over duck. Then cover roaster and place in oven for 3 hours. Baste frequently and add hot water as necessary.

Trout

. . . .

Melt ½ cup butter in iron skillet over medium heat. Roll whole trout or fillets in a mixture of half cornmeal and half flour and lay fish in melted butter. Turn frequently and watch carefully to keep butter from burning. Take out when golden brown.

Baked Fish

. . . .

⅔ cup sour cream	chips
2 teaspoons chili powder	2 pounds fish (any kind of white
2 tablespoons lemon juice	fish)
1½ to 2 cups finely crushed corn	Margarine or butter

Mix together the sour cream, chili powder, and lemon juice. Place half of corn chips in large greased baking dish. Lay fish on top of crumbs, spread sour cream mixture on top of fish. Sprinkle remaining corn chip crumbs on top of this. Drizzle with margarine or butter. Bake at 500° for about 10 minutes or until flaky. Serve hot.

People always want to know about our vacations.

Most people take vacations to get away from it all and enjoy the rest and relaxation that it provides. But in our family this is not always the case. One vacation in particular caused us to rush back to the hassles of everyday living, happy for the chance to escape from each other and vacation.

Our Florida vacation started out as a really exciting trip for me since I love the ocean and I love loafing. The trip started with the frantic rush of last-minute crises that always precede our vacation. Now, Uncle Henry, who is grumpy and impatient and somehow downright hateful when he has to put up with us, was our driver. He was working for Dolly at that time. Even though he was already doing some bus driving, singing, and writing songs for her, he thought taking all of us girls together on a trip was more than he had hired on for. Anyway, he was not in a good mood. This turned out to be the wrong move on his part because when we girls are together we're what our brothers call a "mighty force."

On this vacation we were camping. After we had set up camp, some guys gave us a basket of fish, but only after we promised to clean them ourselves. We did. We tried to get Uncle Henry to help us or at least build a fire. He wouldn't. He said, "I don't catch them, I don't clean them." He thought we were stupid for doing it when we could go to a restaurant and eat. We thought that he was hateful and lazy. We had fish, hush puppies, slaw, and they were wonderful! Stella even fried a pan of potatoes. Uncle Henry was hungry so he filled his plate. Stella looked at me, I looked at Uncle Henry and said, "You don't catch them, clean them, or cook them. I guess you just eat them." Well, all I got for that speech was a sharp kick on my shins under the table from Dolly's high heels.

Baked Raccoon

. . . .

1   raccoon, cut in pieces
1   teaspoon salt
1   tablespoon pepper

1   bay leaf
2   medium apples, chopped
4   strips bacon

Rub raccoon with salt and pepper. Place raccoon in roasting pan. Fill half full of water. Add salt, pepper, and bay leaf. Cover and parboil for 30 minutes. Remove. Place apples in pan with bacon across meat. Bake for 1½ hours at 350°. Baste with drippings. Serve with mashed potatoes and butter beans.

Grandmother Tennessee (Tenny) Russell Parton (my father's grandmother), at age 97, stands among the hills she loved and for which she was named.

Fried Frog Legs

12	frog legs	1½	tablespoons salt
2	cups milk	1½	tablespoons pepper
2	cups vegetable oil	1	lemon, cut in slices
1½	cups flour		

Marinate frog legs in milk for 2 hours. Place oil in skillet and heat to 375°. Drain frog legs. Roll in seasoned flour. Drop in skillet one at a time. Cook until brown. Drain on paper towels. Garnish with lemon.

Pan Broiled Venison

....

1	pound venison steak		Salt
¼	teaspoon Tabasco sauce	2	tablespoons cooking oil

Season steak with Tabasco sauce and salt, then place in heated oil in skillet. Pan broil on one side until nicely browned. Turn and brown on other side. Serve at once with melted butter.

VEGETABLES AND SIDE DISHES

Red Cabbage Cooked with Apples

....

Cut (shred) 2 pounds red cabbage as for cole slaw. Put in kettle, cover with water, add 2 medium sour apples which have been pared and sliced, 1 heaping tablespoon of lard or butter, sugar, and cider vinegar to suit taste. Cook slowly about 1 hour or a little longer. Cabbage should be a deep red when cooked.

Caramel Lima Beans

....

1	cup large dried lima beans	1	teaspoon salt
½	cup sugar	4	strips bacon

Rinse lima beans, add 2½ cups water, and soak for several hours. Then bring to a boil and simmer gently while preparing caramel. Melt sugar in saucepan over moderate heat, stirring until light brown. Pour into boiling beans, add salt. Turn into casserole dish and cover. Bake at 300° for 2½ hours. An hour before serving, uncover, top with strips of bacon, and bake until the beans are tender and bacon delicately browned. Serves 4 to 6 people. Very good with hot dogs or hamburgers for outdoor eating.

Pinto Beans with Cheese

. . . .

1   cup dried pinto beans
3   cups water
1   teaspoon salt
2   slices bacon, cut in small pieces
1   onion, finely sliced
½   green bell pepper, seeded and
     finely chopped

½   pound sharp Cheddar cheese, cut
     in 1-inch cubes
1   fresh tomato, finely chopped
1   tablespoon chili powder
     Ground black pepper

Wash the beans, place beans in water in a large kettle, cover, bring to a boil and simmer for 2 minutes. Remove from heat and let soak 1 hour. Add salt to beans, cover, and simmer for 2 hours, or until beans are tender. Fry bacon until crisp, remove from pan, and sauté onion and green pepper in bacon drippings. Stir in bacon, beans, cheese, tomato, chili powder, and pepper. Cook slowly, stirring constantly for 5 minutes, or until the cheese is melted. Serves 6.

Indian Corn Stew

. . . .

2   tablespoons margarine
1   onion, finely chopped
⅓   cup chopped green pepper
1   pound ground beef
2   to 4 cups fresh corn

1   can tomato soup
2   teaspoons sugar
1½ teaspoons salt
1   tablespoon Worcestershire sauce

Melt margarine in heavy skillet. Add onion and green pepper. Cook until soft. Add meat and brown well, stirring often. Add corn, tomato soup, sugar, salt, and Worcestershire sauce. Simmer 1 hour. Makes 4 to 6 servings.

Dolly wishing she were anywhere other than the (Owens) family-owned sawmill in this one-horse town. Our papa and other family members worked in the timber mills and sawmills.

Fried Rice

1   medium onion, chopped
3   mushrooms, sliced or chopped
1   cup diced cooked meat (pork or chicken)
2   tablespoons vegetable oil

½   teaspoon ground pepper
3   cups cooked cold rice
2   tablespoons soy sauce
1   egg, beaten

Fry onion, mushrooms, and meat together in oil for 10 minutes. Season with pepper. Add rice and soy sauce. Cook for additional 10 minutes. Add beaten egg, mix. Serves about 6.

Baked Beans

4   cups dried pinto beans
1   medium onion, chopped
4   tablespoons dark corn syrup

½   teaspoon salt
⅓   pound salt pork (sliced and fried)

Wash beans thoroughly and soak overnight. In morning, use the same water to cook beans. Boil 1 hour counting from time the water starts to boil, put in bean pot, add onion, syrup, and salt. Place 1 slice of pork in center of beans and put remaining slices on top. Bake in slow oven, about 250°, for 1 hour.

Baked Potatoes

....

Select smooth potatoes of uniform size. Wash and scrub off any dirt. Rub with sweet butter or olive oil and wrap in foil. Prick before placing in oven to bake. Small potatoes take 25 minutes in a 400° oven, medium potatoes take 45 minutes, and large potatoes take 1 hour.

Scalloped Potatoes

....

6	medium potatoes	1	tablespoon butter
1	tablespoon flour	2½	cups milk
	Salt		Grated cheese (optional)
	Pepper		

Peel and slice potatoes and soak in water for 30 minutes. Drain and arrange the slices in a deep baking dish by layers. Sprinkle each layer with flour, salt, and pepper, and dot with butter before covering with the next layer. Pour milk over, then sprinkle with grated cheese if desired. Bake for 1 hour at 450°.

Baked Potatoes and Cheese

....

6	large potatoes (baked)	⅓	cup hot milk
¼	pound pimiento or American cheese, grated	2	teaspoons salt
		⅛	teaspoon paprika

Cut potatoes in half lengthwise and scoop out the centers. Mash thoroughly. Add cheese to hot milk and beat with an egg beater until smooth. Mix with the potatoes, add seasoning, and whip until light and creamy. Refill the potato shells and bake in a 400° oven for 10 minutes.

White Beans, Country Style

1 pound dried white beans	1 green bell pepper, finely chopped
Salt and black pepper	3 fresh tomatoes, peeled and
1 clove garlic, finely chopped	coarsely chopped
1 bay leaf	½ teaspoon dried oregano leaves, or
6 tablespoons butter	fresh if available
2 medium onions, finely chopped	¼ cup fresh parsley, finely chopped

Cover washed beans with 5 cups cold water and soak overnight, covered, in refrigerator. Next day, season to taste with salt and black pepper, add garlic and bay leaf. Bring to boiling point, reduce heat, and simmer, covered, until the beans are tender, about 2 hours. Stir occasionally while beans are cooking. Drain thoroughly.

Place 4 tablespoons butter in a large skillet and sauté onions until golden brown. Add green pepper and tomato and cook 5 minutes. Add the oregano leaves and parsley and blend well. Add to beans with the remainder of butter and stir gently before serving. Serves 4 to 6 people.

Mother and Papa at home in 1996.

Fried Sweet Potatoes

Wash, peel, and slice 2 or 3 sweet potatoes. Fry in hot oil or butter. A sprinkling of sugar may be added when almost done.

Potato Cakes

2 eggs, beaten
4 tablespoons flour
1 small chopped onion

4 or 5 cups leftover mashed
  potatoes
Salt and pepper to taste

Mix ingredients into a stiff batter. Drop by heaping tablespoons into medium-hot bacon grease and fry until brown on both sides, turning once. Serves 8 to 10.

Deep-fried Potatoes

Cut potatoes ½ inch thick. Drop at once into hot fat. Bring the fat to a boil. Shake the slices while cooking. When they puff up and become brown, they are ready to serve.

Potato Chips

Peel the potatoes and slice them very fine. Soak in cold salty water for 1 hour. Shake in a towel to remove the moisture. Put into a frying basket and fry in deep fat to a golden brown. Drain on brown paper and while drying, sprinkle with salt. To freshen stale or moist chips, place in a hot oven a few minutes before serving.

Left to right: *Cassie, Dolly, myself, and Stella enjoy a picnic on Great-Grandpa Jim Owens's farm in 1972. This property is still in the family.*

French Fried Potatoes

Wash, pare, and cut potatoes in long strips ¼ inch by ¼ inch. Stand in cold water. Heat fat to 400°. Blot the potato slices dry in a towel and put a few at a time in the hot fat. Fry for about 5 minutes or until crisp and brown.

Fried Onions

2	or 3 large onions	1	tablespoon melted butter
	Milk	⅔	cup milk
2	eggs	1	cup flour
	Pinch salt		

Peel onions under water, slice into a bowl of milk, let stand 15 minutes, drain, dry with towel. Beat eggs, add salt, butter, ⅔ cup milk, and flour to make smooth batter. Fold in onions, drop battered onions in deep hot fat. Or dip onions in flour and fry.

Fried Onion Rings

. . . .

1   large onion, sliced in ¼-inch
    slices
1   cup all-purpose flour
1   tablespoon cornmeal
2   tablespoons salt

¼   teaspoon black pepper
1½ teaspoons baking powder
1   egg, separated
⅔   cup milk
    Vegetable oil

Separate onion into rings. Place rings in bowl; cover with ice water. Let stand 20 minutes. Drain on paper towel. Mix together flour, cornmeal, salt, pepper, and baking powder in separate bowl. Combine egg yolk, milk, and 1 tablespoon oil. Beat well. Stir egg mixture into flour mixture. Mix well. Beat egg white until stiff, fold into batter. Heat 1 inch of vegetable oil in skillet to 375°. Dip onion rings in batter and deep fry until golden brown for approximately 3 to 5 minutes. Remove and drain on paper towels.

Stuffed Onions

. . . .

6   onions
2   tablespoons chopped bacon
1   apple, chopped
2   cups soft breadcrumbs
¼   teaspoon salt

1   teaspoon grated lemon rind
¼   teaspoon ginger
    Pepper to taste
2   tablespoons ketchup

Peel onions, cover with rapidly boiling salted water. Cook until translucent. Drain. Scoop out the centers. Brown bacon lightly. Add apple, bread, and ½ cup of chopped cooked onions. Season with salt, lemon rind, ginger, and pepper. Fill onion cups. Bake in shallow pan at 375° for 40 minutes. Add 1 teaspoon ketchup to each onion before serving.

Creamed Onions

. . . .

1 pound small white onions	1 cup milk, heated
4 tablespoons butter	½ teaspoon salt
2 tablespoons flour	⅛ teaspoon pepper

To make peeling of onions easier, place them in a pot of boiling water and cook for 2 minutes. Drain and peel. Melt butter and blend in flour; add warm milk gradually, stirring constantly. Reduce heat and cook 3 minutes longer; add seasoning and onions.

Brown Onion Soup

. . . .

1 cup minced onion	3 beef bouillon cubes
3 tablespoons butter or margarine	2 cups boiling water
3 tablespoons flour	1 cup milk
½ teaspoon salt	

Brown onions in butter or margarine. Remove from heat. Add flour and salt. Stir until blended. Combine bouillon cubes and boiling water. Stir until dissolved. Add to onion mixture, cook, stirring constantly, until thickened. Add milk, heat to boiling. Serve hot.

6

Thanksgiving Dinner —All Day Long

In this country, Thanksgiving seems to be pretty much a holiday that most everyone celebrates. With or without religious overtones, we can all gather together to be thankful for our friends and family and the love and memories we share. I think of Thanksgiving as the ultimate harvest feast—somehow a time of bounty and fullness even when times were hard.

I don't remember ever having a roasted turkey or a pot roast until I was grown up. When we kids were little, I remember that we had chicken or pork and even two ducks once. Since the mid-fifties, we have had both—turkey and pot roast— along with other wonderful things like mandarin oranges and candied cherries. We probably overused them, but these were things that we didn't have all the time or everyday—so they were special to us.

Before Thanksgiving, we would gather hickory nuts, walnuts, hazelnuts, and— yes—acorns. Our grandmothers used to make a bread with acorns and beans. Once, after I was grown, I asked Mother how to make that bread, and she said, "Oh, child, you don't need to make things like that now." Don't *need* to—but I wanted to and did—I used chestnuts instead, though.

Often, we gathered walnuts by the sackful. We used to draw and paint with the plants and berries and barks that we would gather—especially in the fall.

We had different kinds of apple trees: "striped June," a winter "small John" and "sour John" (pale yellow, cooking apples), a sweet apple that stayed green-white, and "fox apples." We made apple pies, apple cakes, apple dumplings, apple butter, apple jelly, and apple cider. The apples were "free," and so we used them and used them and used them.

Fixing Thanksgiving dinner was an all-day project. The visiting was just about as important as the cooking. As a family, we drew on what we had to make our "feast," and we didn't think about whether we had less than some others might have. We had what we had, but most important—we had each other. And that—always—was what all of us were most thankful for. We all tried to contribute what we could to the building of the dinner. And that was what made it special. Dinner would have to be different every year because we did have to "make do." But as we moved from hard times to less hard times that aspect of our all-day Thanksgiving dinner never changed because it was the most important part.

When all of the Partons and Owenses get together for a family reunion, as we do every year, there are so many of us that the camera can't get all of us in.

MAIN DISHES

Roast Chicken

Clean and stuff chicken (use any dressing desired), fasten legs, place chicken in baking pan, rub well with salt and a little pepper. Spread chicken with soft butter, place in oven 20 minutes at 450°. Then reduce heat to 350°. Baste chicken every 10 minutes using boiling water and a little butter. Add a little boiled water to bottom of pan. Bake 2 hours if 4 pound chicken. To glaze surface, brush chicken with soft butter and brown.

Hot Turkey and Cheese Sandwich with Icing (Spread)

1 turkey breast, cooked and chopped	½ cup ripe olives, chopped
4 boiled eggs, chopped	⅔ cup mayonnaise
½ cup celery, chopped	Bread

Combine above ingredients and spread on rounds of bread with crust trimmed. Make each sandwich with 3 slices of bread. Ice each sandwich with following mixture.

Icing for Sandwich:

2 small jars sharp cheese spread	1 egg, beaten
1 cup margarine	

Mix above ingredients at room temperature until fluffy. Spread mixture on top of sandwiches. Refrigerate sandwiches after icing for 24 hours. Bake on ungreased cookie sheet for 15 to 20 minutes at 375°. Makes 8 sandwiches.

All the fattening food we love to eat didn't seem to hurt Dolly much.

Fast Curry from Leftovers

Chop and sauté 1 onion and 1 rib celery in 2 tablespoons butter until tender. Add 1 to 2 tablespoons curry powder, 3 tablespoons flour, ¼ teaspoon ginger and cook, stirring, 1 minute. Gradually add 2 cups water or leftover broth and bring to boil, stirring, and cook 2 minutes. Add 3 cups leftover cooked, diced meat, poultry, or vegetables. Salt to taste. Serve with rice. (I always use broth or leftover gravy, which makes it better.)

VEGETABLES AND SIDE DISHES

Turnips in Sugar

Scrape and dice 4 cups turnips, boil in salted water until they are tender. Make a thick sauce of two tablespoons flour cooked in 2 tablespoons butter, add 1 cup of milk, 3 tablespoons sugar, and season to taste. Cook until thick, add to turnips, and simmer for about 10 minutes.

Fried Turnips

Peel and slice 4 turnips, rinse in cold water. While still damp, sprinkle heavily with flour, salt, and pepper. Fry in hot oil until light brown and tender. Potatoes are good the same way or mix them, 2 potatoes and 2 turnips.

Turnips

3 cups turnips	¼ teaspoon paprika
½ teaspoon salt	¼ teaspoon pepper

Wash, peel, and cut turnips in quarters. Cook uncovered in boiling salted water until tender. Drain, mash, and just before serving add salt, paprika, pepper, and butter, or serve quartered. I use equal amounts of turnips and potatoes.

Baked Squash

Split acorn or winter squash in two lengthwise. Remove the seeds and place in a pan shell-side up. Bake at 300° for 2 hours or until soft. Remove the pulp from the shell, mash to remove any lumps and season with pepper and salt. Mix in 2 teaspoons butter.

In the fall we gathered hickory nuts, walnuts, and hazelnuts. We used them to cook with, as well as for treats. We'd sit for hours cracking enough to use. Papa always cooked and then roasted pig tails, pig ears, and pig feet. He introduced the older children to this unusual food while they were very young. Mother would not touch it. We thought it was great because Papa said so.

Freezer Slaw

1 medium head of cabbage, grated	1 green pepper
1 teaspoon salt	1 carrot

Grate pepper and carrot and set aside.

Put 1 teaspoon salt on the grated cabbage and let stand 1 hour. Then squeeze all the liquid out.

While cabbage is soaking make syrup of:

1 cup cider vinegar	½ teaspoon mustard seed and 1
2 cups white sugar	teaspoon celery seed in cloth bag
¼ cup water	

Combine vinegar, sugar, and water. Drop bag of seed in syrup. Bring to boil and boil 1 minute. Let stand to lukewarm, pour over cabbage, carrots, and green peppers. Place in freezer. To use, just thaw.

This is a good and quick way to use up the end-of-season cabbages and have crunchy slaw in the middle of winter.

Apple Rings

3 medium apples	⅓ lemon, sliced
1 cup sugar	½ teaspoon red food coloring
¾ cup water	

Cut apples crosswise into rings, leaving skin, and core. Boil sugar, water, and lemon until syrup thickens. Add coloring, blend in apples. Skim out rings after 10 minutes. Serve cold.

Sweet Potato Casserole

3 cups sweet potatoes, cooked and mashed	2 teaspoons salt
1 cup sugar	2 eggs, lightly beaten
½ cup milk	1 teaspoon vanilla extract

Mix together and pour in 12x6x1-inch baking dish. Add topping.

Topping:

⅓ cup melted butter	½ cup flour
1 cup brown sugar	1 cup chopped pecans

Combine in order. Sprinkle over potatoes. Bake at 350° for 30 minutes.

BREADS

Pumpkin Muffins

2 eggs	1 teaspoon cinnamon
1 cup sugar	½ tablespoon baking soda
¾ cup vegetable oil	1 teaspoon baking powder
1 cup pumpkin	½ teaspoon salt
1½ cups flour	1 cup raisins

Beat eggs. Add sugar, oil, and pumpkin, and beat. In sifter, put flour, cinnamon, soda, baking powder, and salt. Sift these ingredients over other mixture. Blend until smooth, then stir in raisins. Fill muffin pans ⅔ full. Bake at 400° for 15 minutes or until done. Freezes well.

Yeast Bread

1 yeast cake dissolved in ½ cup warm water with 1 tablespoon sugar	3 tablespoons sugar
	3 tablespoons shortening
	2 tablespoons salt
4 cups warm water	12 cups self-rising flour

When yeast foams in the water, mix it with 4 cups water, sugar, shortening, and salt. Add flour to make a stiff dough, knead 10 minutes. Put in big greased pan, let rise 2 hours. Punch down and turn over and let rise 1 hour. Put in 3 loaf pans. Let rise 1 hour more. Bake 20 minutes at 350°.

Pumpkin Spice Loaf

3 cups sifted all-purpose flour	4 eggs
2 teaspoons baking powder	1½ cups sugar
2 teaspoons baking soda	½ cup corn syrup
1 teaspoon salt	1 cup vegetable oil
2 teaspoons cinnamon	2 cups canned pumpkin
1½ teaspoons ginger	1 cup raisins
1 teaspoon nutmeg	1 cup chopped nuts
1 teaspoon cloves	

Sift together the flour, baking powder, baking soda, salt, and spices.

In large bowl, beat eggs till light, gradually adding sugar.

Add corn syrup, oil, pumpkin, and beat well. Remove beaters and fold in sifted flour mixture until batter is smooth.

Add raisins and ¾ cup chopped nuts.

Line 2 9x5-inch pans with buttered wax paper and turn batter into them. Sprinkle tops with remaining nuts.

Bake at 325° about 65 minutes, test for doneness with toothpick. Loaves may crack a little on top but no harm.

Chestnut Bread

. . . .

1 *pound chestnuts*
   Cornmeal
   Boiling water (just enough to
   make paste)

Green fodder, green corn shucks,
or tamale papers
White twine

Peel chestnuts, scale to peel off the inside skin, and crush with a fork. Add enough cornmeal to hold chestnuts together, mixing chestnuts and cornmeal with boiling water. Wrap in green fodder or green corn shucks (tamale papers are what I use), tying each bun securely with white twine. Place in a pot of boiling water and cook 2 hours. Salt when eating if desired. Makes 5 or 6 buns.

Bean bread can be made the same way, but cook beans 30 minutes or more before adding cornmeal.

Grandpa Jake and Grandma Rena Owens, my mother's
parents.

Cornmeal Muffins

4 tablespoons shortening	2 teaspoons baking powder
2 tablespoons sugar	½ teaspoon salt
1 egg	1 cup cornmeal
1 cup flour	1¼ cups milk

Cream shortening and sugar. Add well-beaten egg. Sift together flour, baking powder, and salt and mix with cornmeal. Mix wet and dry ingredients together. Add milk gradually. Beat well. Bake in well-greased muffin pans in hot oven (450°) about 25 minutes.

Spicy Thanksgiving Corn Bread

½ cup chopped onions	2 eggs, lightly beaten
½ cup bell pepper, chopped	1 cup whole milk
1 hot pepper, chopped	1½ cups cornmeal
1 cup grated Cheddar cheese	1 7-ounce can creamed corn
½ cup vegetable oil	

Mix. Pour batter into pan. Bake at 350° for 45 minutes.

DRESSINGS AND STUFFINGS

Sage Stuffing

½ pound butter	3 eggs, beaten
2½ teaspoons sage	8 cups fresh breadcrumbs
2½ teaspoons salt	2 cups finely chopped onions
1 teaspoon coarsely ground pepper	2 cups finely chopped celery

Melt butter and add all seasonings. Beat eggs until fluffy. Add eggs to bread, onion, and celery. Add melted butter and mix again. Stuff bird very lightly. Do not put too much stuffing into the cavity.

Chicken Dressing

1	pound pork sausage	1½	teaspoons sage
6	to 8 cups of breadcrumbs (corn bread)	⅔	teaspoon thyme
1	large onion, chopped	2	large eggs or 3 small eggs, beaten
1	cup chopped celery	2½	teaspoons salt
1	teaspoon garlic salt or 2 cloves of garlic, chopped	1½	teaspoons ground black pepper
		3	cups broth

Crumble sausage and cook slowly until brown. Drain off fat. Mix all ingredients, using as much broth as needed to blend well, and stuff large hen or bake on the side as a side dish.

Corn Bread Stuffing

1½	cups mushrooms, chopped	¾	teaspoon marjoram
2	teaspoons margarine	¼	teaspoon mace
1	medium onion, chopped	5	boiled eggs, chopped
1	cup celery, chopped	1	teaspoon salt
3	cups corn bread, crumbled	1	teaspoon pepper
1	teaspoon nutmeg	2	cups pecans, chopped
4	tablespoons parsley flakes	1	14-ounce can chicken bouillon
½	teaspoon thyme		

Sauté mushrooms in 1 teaspoon margarine. In separate pan, sauté onion and celery in remaining margarine. Mix mushrooms, onion, and celery with next 10 ingredients. Add enough bouillon to blend well. Should be lumpy. Stuff inside cavity of turkey and roast as desired.

Chestnut Stuffing

2 cups seedless raisins	½ cup heavy cream
3½ cups chestnut meats	1 cup breadcrumbs
¼ cup butter, melted	½ teaspoon onion seasoning
1 teaspoon salt	½ teaspoon celery salt
Dash pepper	

Cook raisins in a little water about 10 minutes and drain. Cook chestnuts in boiling water until soft. Drain, rinse, and mash. Add remaining ingredients and mix well.

Lillie Owens Huskey, my mother's aunt and Grandpa Jake's sister, had a lot of influence on the older children in our family. She helped teach us to cook, can, and sew, and she always told us to stand up for what we thought was right and never to let anyone mistreat us. She still makes birthday cakes for my son, Mitchell.

Thanksgiving Persimmon Pudding

1 quart very ripe persimmons
1 medium sweet potato, baked and peeled
1 tablespoon sugar

3 tablespoons flour
3 or 4 tablespoons butter, melted
2 eggs, well-beaten
1 pint light cream

Put persimmons and sweet potato through sieve to remove seeds and skin from persimmons. Mix sugar, flour, butter, and eggs. Add cream, a little at a time, until all cream is added. Pour this mixture into persimmon and potato mixture. Mix well. Pour into a buttered baking dish. Bake at 300° for 30 minutes. Serve with a sweet dip.

Thanksgiving Pumpkin Pie

2 cups cooked pumpkin, well-drained, or 1 16-ounce can pumpkin
1 14-ounce can Eagle brand milk
2 eggs

½ teaspoon nutmeg
1 teaspoon cinnamon
½ teaspoon salt
½ teaspoon ginger
1 9-inch unbaked pie shell

Preheat oven to 425°. In large bowl, combine pumpkin, milk, eggs, and spices. Mix well and turn into pie shell. Bake for 15 minutes, reduce oven to 350°, and continue baking for an additional 35 to 40 minutes or until knife inserted 1 inch from edge comes out clean. Cool thoroughly before cutting.

Super Simple Carrot Cake

2	cups sugar	4	eggs, lightly beaten
3	cups flour	1	cup vegetable oil
½	teaspoon salt	3	junior size (2-inch) baby carrots, grated
2	teaspoons baking powder		
2	teaspoons baking soda	1	cup chopped nuts
2	teaspoons cinnamon	1	cup golden raisins

Mix all ingredients well, adding nuts and raisins last. Pour into greased and floured 10-inch tube pan. Bake at 350° for 1 hour. Cool and frost with cream cheese frosting.

Cream Cheese Frosting:

1	8-ounce package cream cheese	2	cups powdered sugar
3	tablespoons soft margarine		Yellow food coloring
1	tablespoon milk (can use a bit more if desired)	½	cup almonds, finely chopped (optional)
½	teaspoon vanilla extract		

Mix together cream cheese, margarine, milk, and vanilla. Stir in powdered sugar. I usually add a few drops of yellow food coloring. This makes the frosting soft enough to drizzle over cake and makes it a beautiful yellow color. Then I sprinkle frosting with finely chopped nuts.

Spicy Ginger Cupcakes

1	cup flour	1	teaspoon cinnamon
½	cup sugar	¾	teaspoon baking powder
⅓	cup shortening	¾	teaspoon baking soda
⅓	cup molasses	½	teaspoon ginger
1	egg	¼	teaspoon nutmeg

In medium bowl with mixer at low speed, beat all ingredients and ½ cup water. Increase speed to high. Beat 2 minutes, scraping sides of bowl occasionally. Place 2 level tablespoons of dough in greased muffin tins or paper liners. Bake at 350° for 15 to 20 minutes. Makes 16 cupcakes.

Butterscotch Pie with Brown Sugar Meringue

3 eggs, separated (reserve whites for meringue)
1 cup brown sugar
6 level tablespoons flour
½ teaspoon nutmeg
2 cups milk

¼ teaspoon salt
3 tablespoons caramel syrup (recipe follows)
4 tablespoons butter
1 teaspoon vanilla
1 pie shell, baked

Beat egg yolks with sugar and nutmeg, mix flour with a little water to make smooth paste, add to first mixture, add milk, salt, and caramel syrup. Cook in double boiler until thick. Remove from heat, add butter and vanilla. Cool. Pour into baked crust. Top with brown sugar meringue and bake at 325° for 15 to 18 minutes or until brown.

Caramel Syrup:
½ cup sugar

⅓ cup boiling water

To make syrup, heat sugar in smooth dry skillet until golden brown. Add boiling water. Cook until creamy.

Brown Sugar Meringue:
3 egg whites (reserved from pie filling)
4 tablespoons light brown sugar, firmly packed

½ teaspoon vanilla extract

Beat egg whites until frothy. Add sugar gradually and beat until stiff. Add vanilla.

Not everyone is always excited about our singings and dinners. Cassie's daughter, Rebecca, decided to sleep through the party we had at Dolly's home in Sevier County.

Chocolate Bread Pudding with Cream Sauce

2 cups stale breadcrumbs	2 eggs
4 cups milk	⅔ cup sugar
½ teaspoon nutmeg	½ teaspoon salt
⅓ cup cocoa	

Put bread, milk, nutmeg, and cocoa in bowl. Soak 2 or 3 minutes. Beat eggs; add sugar and salt. Mash soaked crumbs, add egg mixture, and mix well. Pour into pudding dish, set in hot water, and bake in oven (250° to 275°) about 40 minutes. Serve with cream sauce.

Cream Sauce:

1 egg, separated	½ teaspoon vanilla
⅓ cup milk	½ pint cream
⅓ cup sugar	

Beat egg white until stiff, add milk, beaten yolk, and sugar. Add vanilla, then cream. Cook in double boiler until just hot.

Apple Butter Pie

½ cup brown sugar	½ cup milk
2 egg yolks, slightly beaten	1½ cups water
½ cup apple butter	1 tablespoon unflavored gelatin
½ teaspoon salt	2 tablespoons granulated sugar
1½ teaspoons cinnamon	2 cups whipped cream
½ teaspoon nutmeg	1 pie shell, baked
⅛ teaspoon cloves	

Combine brown sugar, egg yolks, apple butter, salt, spices, milk, and 1 cup water. Cook until smooth and thick, stirring constantly. Soften gelatin in ½ cup water. Add to hot mixture. Stir until dissolved. Cool until partly set. Beat until light and fluffy. Fold sugar into whipped cream. Fold into gelatin mixture. Pour into baked pastry shell. Chill.

Apple Noodle Pudding

½ cup raisins	2 apples, peeled, cored, and diced
½ cup apple juice or cider	1 teaspoon lemon juice
1 12-ounce package wide egg noodles	4 eggs, well beaten
	Salt and pepper to taste
¼ pound unsalted margarine, melted	½ teaspoon cinnamon
	½ cup sugar

Soak raisins in apple juice or cider for 1 hour or overnight.

Cook noodles in boiling water until tender (5 to 10 minutes). Drain. Combine margarine, apples, lemon juice, and drained raisins in large bowl. Add eggs. Mix well. Add noodles. Season to taste with salt and pepper.

Spoon into well-oiled 9x13-inch baking dish. Sprinkle with cinnamon and sugar. Bake at 375° for 45 minutes until top is brown and crisp. Cut into squares, serve hot or cold. Very good.

Old Country Apple Cake

(Great-Great Grandmother's recipe, probably late 1800s)

Dough:

1½	sticks butter	2	heaping tablespoons sour cream
1	cup sugar	3	cups sifted flour
3	eggs	2	tablespoons baking powder

Cream butter and sugar, add eggs, sour cream, flour, and baking powder. Add small amounts of flour as needed to make dough. Press half of dough in baking dish.

Filling (I usually double this):

4	small apples (tart)	1	tablespoon lemon juice
1	cup white raisins (soaked in 2 cups cold water)	½	cup sugar
			Cinnamon and nutmeg to taste

Grate apples, add drained raisins, lemon juice, and sugar. Spoon evenly over dough. Sprinkle cinnamon and nutmeg over mixture.

Cover with remaining dough; press into pan with spatula or by hand. Sprinkle cinnamon and sugar on top. Dot generously with butter. Bake at 300° for 2 hours until light golden brown. Cut in squares while warm.

Store in cake or cookie tins. Keeps well.

Fall of the year, when the mornings are crisp and late afternoons are for long walks, because it's the first time we can enjoy walking without the heat. Then the food preparations take over. Foods that can be enjoyed around the campfire or at the dinner table; rich and creamy soups; the aroma of homemade breads; the last of the garden treasures—fried cabbage, creamed corn, pumpkin, and always sweet potatoes; the last of the tomatoes; and wonderful apples and the many dishes we can make with them. We always have what are called "naked cakes"—a spicy cake with no icing—gingerbreads, and dark, warm shortbreads. We use a lot of macaroni, tomatoes, and beans for soup and stews. Now, I look forward to frosty mornings and cool nights, putting on extra layers of clothing and having a toasty fire in the fireplace and hearty, rich foods—full of vitamins, and laden with calories, spices, and flavor.

Red River Apple Pie

⅓ cup cinnamon candy (red hots)	½ teaspoon nutmeg
½ cup sugar	⅓ teaspoon salt
½ cup hot water	1 tablespoon lemon juice
6 cups sliced green apples with peel	2 tablespoons butter
¼ cup flour	1 pie shell, unbaked
½ cup sugar	

Melt candy and sugar in water. Combine apples, flour, sugar, nutmeg, and salt. Add lemon juice to cinnamon syrup and pour over apples. Blend until apples are coated with syrup. Pour into a 10-inch shallow frying pan or baking pan. Dot with butter. Place a pastry crust over apples and trim edge. Seal by moistening edge of dish and press in crust. Bake at 450° for 10 minutes, then lower heat to 350° and continue baking for 40 or 50 minutes, until apples are tender. Baste crust with butter during the last 10 minutes.

Chocolate Chip Chess Pie

¼ cup mini chocolate chips	1 tablespoon cornmeal
1 pie shell, unbaked	1 tablespoon apple cider vinegar
3 eggs, lightly beaten	1 teaspoon vanilla extract
1¾ cups sugar	¼ cup butter, melted
¾ cup evaporated milk	

Line unbaked pie shell with chocolate chips. Mix remaining ingredients by hand or with wire whip and pour slowly over chocolate chips in pie shell. Bake 1 hour at 350°.

—From the files of the former Nobles Restaurant in Brentwood, Tennessee

Easy Cake

½ cup butter	1½ cups flour
1 cup sugar	2 teaspoons baking powder
2 eggs	¼ teaspoon salt
1 teaspoon vanilla extract	1 cup milk

Cream butter, sugar, eggs, and vanilla. Mix flour, baking powder, and salt together. Add to egg mixture alternately with milk. Pour into 2 greased cake pans and bake 30 minutes at 325° to 350°. Cool and ice with caramel frosting.

Caramel Frosting:

1 stick margarine	1 1-pound box powdered sugar, sifted
1 cup brown sugar, packed	
¼ cup milk	1 teaspoon vanilla extract

Melt margarine and brown sugar over low heat. Boil 2 minutes, remove from heat. Add milk, return to heat. Bring to boil again. Remove from heat, add sifted powdered sugar and vanilla, mix well. If too stiff, add more milk. Beat with mixer.

7

Christmas Dinner at Our House

You all are probably getting tired of me talking about hard times. Well, I can't stop because it's true and that's how we grew up. But I'm not complaining about it—at all. Hard times were just a fact of life, and I'm not sure just how aware we kids were really.

Within the family, "things"—or the lack of them—weren't particularly important. Other people—sometimes in kindness, sometimes in cruelty—might remind us from time to time that we had fewer material things than many. I imagine most of you know the story of Dolly's "coat of many colors." Well, she was always proud of it because she knew the love that went into making it, and if some of her schoolmates didn't understand that, well, they were the poorer for it—not us.

Anyway, how we kids understood Christmas and how our family celebrated it was a product of hard times in east Tennessee. And I don't feel a bit deprived.

We kids were older before we ever had "real" ice cream. But we had snow ice cream every winter, and in my memory—even now—that's still the best.

We made potato candy for as long as I can remember, and we made molasses candy and honey candy and fudge. At Christmas, stick candy and oranges were very special treats. I remember the first time I tasted orange soda and a cola drink. Some neighbors had relatives who lived off somewhere in a "city," and they brought some "soda pop" with them when they visited. I remember them telling us that they had these drinks all the time—we kids talked about that and decided we didn't believe them. This must be something they had only because they were on "vacation."

But not having much and feeling "deprived" are two different things. And we didn't have much—especially around Christmas. That was why Christmas dinner was so special. But I don't think any of us kids ever felt that we were missing out on anything important.

I remember coconuts being a part of the holidays a couple of times. Real coconuts. I can remember what a treat it was to be around when holes were made in the "eyes" of the coconut to drain the milk out and what a treat it was to get to drink some of the "milk." And the smell when the nut was cracked open and those little tastes of the fresh coconut meat we would sneak—oh, will I ever be simple again?

It still reminds me—for some reason—of what we used to do for our cats. Of course, we had our own milk cow. We made having to get up in the freeze of early winter mornings a little better by another "milk ritual." We always fed the cats warm milk as soon as we had milked the cow. Mother would take a dipper full out of the bucket and pour it into the cats' pan. The cats got the morning "leftovers" too: gravy and bits of biscuit. Our dogs got the leftovers in the evenings; I'm sure the cats preferred that since they never seemed too fond of vegetables and corn bread. Now my cats have come to expect the warm cup of milk I fix for them now—except it's warmed in a microwave, not in the cow.

I guess that's part of what I mean. "Things" change, and so they don't really matter. It's the people and creatures we love that are constant, and that's what I remember about Christmas and Christmas dinner at our house.

MAIN DISHES

Fried Chicken

1 pint buttermilk
1 teaspoon salt
¼ teaspoon black pepper
3 eggs

1 chicken, cut up (2 1/2 pounds)
Flour
Vegetable oil

Mix milk, salt, pepper, and eggs together. Pour over chicken, let set for 2 or 3 hours. Then roll in flour and fry in oil about 30 minutes.

Chicken and Dressing Casserole

5 boneless chicken breasts
1 14-ounce can chicken broth
2 10-ounce cans cream-of-chicken-and-broccoli soup

1 8-ounce container sour cream
1 bag herb stuffing mix

Bake or stew chicken breasts until completely cooked, then cool. After cooling break into pieces. Then lay chicken in bottom of sheet cake pan or long casserole dish. Mix soup and sour cream together and pour over chicken, pour stuffing mix over soup and sour cream, and then pour broth over stuffing mix. Put casserole in oven to brown the top, about 15 to 20 minutes. Bake at 350° to 375° for about 30 minutes.

VEGETABLES AND SIDE DISHES

Parsley Potatoes

Cut cold boiled potatoes into slices, season with salt and pepper. Slice an onion and fry in 2 tablespoons butter or beef fat. Have the butter very hot and turn in the potatoes. Cook until the potatoes have taken in the fat and serve with chopped parsley.

Baked Sweet Potatoes

Wash, peel, and slice enough sweet potatoes to cover shallow glass baking dish. Bake thoroughly at 350°, remove from oven, and cover with a layer of marshmallows. Put back in oven for a few minutes until brown. Serve hot.

Pimiento Potatoes

6 medium potatoes
Salt
Chopped pimientos

Onion juice
Pepper

Wash, pare, and dice potatoes. Shake dry in a towel. Fry in hot fat and drain on brown paper. Sprinkle with salt. Just before serving, put the pimientos, a few drops of onion juice, and pepper in a frying pan, add the potatoes, and cook together. Keep shaking the potatoes so that they do not stick to pan.

Dolly's Dill Dumplings

(From Stella's cookbook *Really Cooking*)

2 cups cholesterol-free Bisquick
1 cup milk
1 teaspoon dill

1 tablespoon sugar
½ stick butter, melted

Mix together and drop by tablespoon into boiling stew such as stewed tomatoes, potatoes, beef, or chicken. It doesn't matter, just whatever type of stew you want. Sprinkle a bit more dill on top of the dumplings. Cover and let cook about 10 minutes on medium heat. Serve hot.

Pink and Rhoda Lewis were neighbors of ours when we were growing up.

Cranberry Bean Succotash

1 pound dried cranberry beans
1 46-ounce can tomato juice
2 teaspoons salt
2 tablespoons butter
1 12-ounce can baby lima beans
1 green bell pepper, seeded and finely chopped
2 fresh tomatoes, medium size, coarsely chopped
1 12-ounce can whole kernel corn
2 tablespoons fresh parsley, finely chopped
1 onion, finely chopped
1 clove garlic, finely chopped
  Salt and ground black pepper
½ cup grated Parmesan cheese

Wash the beans, then put in large kettle with tomato juice, bring to boil, and simmer 2 minutes. Remove from heat and let soak 1 hour. Add salt and butter and simmer gently for 3 hours, or until beans are tender. In a greased 3-quart casserole dish, mix together the cooked beans, lima beans, green pepper, tomatoes, corn, parsley, onions, garlic, salt, and pepper to taste. Sprinkle the top with grated cheese. Bake at 350°, uncovered, for 30 minutes or until the cheese is delicately browned. Serves 12.

Chestnuts in Hot Cream Sauce

1 pound chestnuts	1½ cups cream
1 tablespoon butter, melted	Pepper
1 tablespoon flour	Paprika

Simmer peeled chestnuts 1 hour in salted water. After thoroughly draining chestnuts, put them into hot cream sauce.

To make cream sauce, add flour to melted butter and cook over medium heat 1 to 2 minutes. Slowly add cream. Cook until thickened. Season with pepper and paprika.

Shrimp Snacks

1 6-ounce can cocktail shrimp	Salt
1 tablespoon horseradish	Dash of grated lemon peel
6 ounces cream cheese, softened	Bread (white or whole wheat)
Dash of Tabasco	

Drain shrimp; mash with a fork. Add remaining ingredients (except bread). Mix together thoroughly.

Take slices of bread, cut 9 squares, 1 inch in size. Let bread sit out for ½ hour. Put spread on each cube of bread. Stick under broiler for 1 to 2 minutes, until light golden brown. Serve hot.

Spread can also be put on cubes of bread and put into refrigerator until ready to broil.

Cole Slaw

1 medium head cabbage, chopped	1 tablespoon salt
1 medium onion, chopped	¼ cup cider vinegar
1 small bell pepper, chopped	1 cup salad dressing or mayonnaise
½ cup sugar	

Mix all ingredients together in large bowl. Refrigerate for 4 hours before serving. Lift slaw out of juice and drain before serving.

Holiday Lime Mold

1 20½-ounce can pineapple tidbits
1 3-ounce package lime Jell-O
1 cup evaporated milk
¾ cup diced red apple

½ cup chopped nuts
½ cup mayonnaise or salad dressing
1 tablespoon lemon juice

Drain syrup from pineapple (reserve juice); add enough water to syrup to make 1 cup; then heat. Dissolve Jell-O in hot syrup; cool slightly and stir in evaporated milk. Chill until as thick as unbeaten egg whites. Fold in pineapple, apple, nuts, mayonnaise, and lemon juice. Pour into a 5½-cup mold. Chill until firm. Unmold on lettuce. Serves 6 to 8.

Note: Grease mold with vegetable oil before pouring in the gelatin mixture. It will unmold more easily.

BREADS

Cinnamon Bread

½ cup butter
2 eggs, beaten
1 cup flour

½ teaspoon ground cinnamon
1 cup milk
   Powdered sugar

Melt butter in heavy iron 12-inch skillet or 8x8-inch baking dish. Mix eggs, flour, cinnamon, and milk to a rough consistency and pour mixture over butter in skillet. Bake in preheated oven at 375° or 400° for 20 minutes. Sprinkle powdered sugar on top and serve for breakfast with syrup, jelly, or jam. Serves 4. This is also a wonderful pancake mix.

Broccoli Bread with Filling

Thaw 2 loaves frozen bread dough, let rise, and shape the two loaves together. Roll dough into a rectangle approximately 10x18 inches.

Lay slices of mozzarella cheese down the center of the loaf, sprinkle with Parmesan cheese, add broccoli mixture on top of cheese. Add more Parmesan cheese and another layer of mozzarella cheese. Starting at center of loaf, pull dough up over filling and pinch together, continue to complete loaf. Flip over onto cookie sheet, seam must be down. Bake at 350° for 30 minutes. When you remove it from the oven, rub butter over the top of the loaf.

Broccoli Filling:

2 10-ounce packages frozen, chopped broccoli
1 medium onion, chopped
1 cup sliced green olives
½ cup chopped mushrooms (optional)
   Salt and pepper to taste
⅓ to ½ cup Italian salad dressing

Combine ingredients and cook approximately 8 minutes. Cool and drain extremely well.

Yeast Rolls

1 pint milk
½ cup shortening
½ cup sugar
6 cups White Lily flour
½ teaspoon baking soda
1 teaspoon salt
1 teaspoon baking powder
2 packets Fleischmann's yeast
½ cup warm water
   Butter

Bring milk to a boil, mix in shortening and sugar. Sift flour. Mix together baking soda, salt, and baking powder, and mix into flour.

Dissolve yeast in warm water. Pour into warm milk mixture and add to flour mixture. Add enough flour to make easily handled dough and let stand in warm place for 30 minutes. Pour dough onto floured pastry sheet. Do not knead. Cut, dip in butter, and place on cookie sheet. Let rise 30 minutes. Bake at 350° until done. Dough can be refrigerated.

Sweet Potato Biscuits

2 cups flour

2 cups cooked, mashed sweet
   potatoes

½ cup molasses

3 tablespoons butter, melted

1½ teaspoons salt

1 teaspoon baking powder

1 cup milk

Mix flour, cooked mashed potatoes, molasses, butter, salt, baking powder. Add milk. Mix, roll out on floured surface, cut, and bake on greased pan 10 to 12 minutes at 350°.

Mother always wanted to have a special cedar tree for Christmas. Rachel and Randy are cutting a Christmas tree.

Christmas Mincemeat Bread

2 cups sifted flour
4 teaspoons baking powder
1 teaspoon salt
1 egg, beaten

½ cup milk
½ cup brown sugar, firmly packed
3 tablespoons melted shortening
1 cup prepared moist mincemeat

Combine and sift flour, baking powder, and salt. Combine egg, milk, sugar, shortening, and mincemeat. Add to flour mixture. Stir only until dry ingredients are moistened. Bake in greased 9½x5½x4-inch loaf pan for 1 hour at 350°. Let stand 24 hours before slicing.

DESSERTS, CANDY, AND BEVERAGES

Snow Balls

1 stick butter
¼ cup sugar
2 cups self-rising flour
2 egg yolks

1 teaspoon vanilla extract
1 cup chopped nut meats
¼ cup water
Powdered sugar

Combine all ingredients thoroughly, except powdered sugar. Form into 1-inch balls. Bake at 350° for 12 minutes. Do not brown. Cool. Roll in powdered sugar.

Molasses Crisps

1¼ cups flour
¾ teaspoon baking soda
½ teaspoon ginger

½ cup molasses
¼ cup shortening

Sift the dry ingredients together. In a saucepan bring molasses and shortening to a boil. Cool slightly. Add flour mixture. Mix well. Chill thoroughly. Roll out and cut in desired shapes. Arrange on greased cookie sheet. Bake at 375° until done, about 8 to 10 minutes. Makes about 2 dozen.

Randy and David's grandson Jordan at my house for a Christmas dinner.

Raisin Pudding

First mixture:

⅓	cup brown sugar	1	cup flour
2	teaspoons baking powder		Pinch salt
¾	cup raisins	½	cup milk

Mix and pour into a greased loaf pan or baking dish.

Second Mixture:

2 teaspoons butter, melted   1 teaspoon vanilla extract

Mix and pour slowly over first mixture and bake at 350° for 1 hour.

Hannah (Rachel's daughter), Rebecca (Cassie's daughter), my father, and Jordan (David's grandson) outside my parents' home in Sevierville.

Gingerbread Boys

1 cup shortening	5 cups flour
1 cup sugar	1½ teaspoons baking soda
½ teaspoon salt	1 tablespoon ground ginger
1 cup molasses	1 teaspoon ground cinnamon
2 tablespoons white vinegar	1 teaspoon ground cloves
1 egg, beaten	

Cream shortening, sugar, and salt. Stir in molasses, vinegar, and egg. Sift together remaining ingredients and add. Chill mixture overnight. Divide dough into fourths. Roll one part of dough at a time on floured board to ¼-inch thickness. Refrigerate remainder. Cut out gingerbread boys with sharp cookie cutter. Place on greased cookie sheets and bake at 375° for about 6 minutes. Cool slightly and remove. Decorate as desired.

White Moon Cake

⅔ cup butter or lard
2 cups sugar
3 cups flour
½ teaspoon salt

3 teaspoons baking powder
1 cup milk
1 teaspoon vanilla
5 egg whites, stiffly beaten

Cream lard until soft and beat in sugar until light and creamy. Sift flour, then resift with salt and baking powder. Add to lard and sugar mixture alternately with milk. Stir in vanilla. Fold in egg whites. Bake in a greased 13x9-inch pan for 25 minutes at 375°. Allow to cool on wire rack.

Moon Glow Lemon Frosting:

Rind of 1 lemon, grated
4 teaspoons lemon juice

2 egg yolks
4½ cups powdered sugar

Add lemon rind and juice to egg yolks. Stir in sugar until right consistency to spread. Frost cake.

Stack Pie (Cake)

4 cups flour
1 teaspoon salt
½ teaspoon baking soda
2 teaspoons baking powder
¾ cup shortening

1 cup sugar
1 cup sorghum molasses
3 eggs
1 cup milk
3 cups applesauce

Sift well flour, salt, soda, and baking powder. Cream shortening, then add sugar a little at a time, blending well. Add sorghum and mix thoroughly. Add eggs one at a time, beating well until smooth, add milk. Pour ⅓ inch deep in 6 or 7 greased 9-inch pans and bake at 300° until a tester comes clean. This will make 6 or 7 layers. When cool, stack layers using sweetened, slightly spiced applesauce as filling.

Cherry Cheesecake

1   8-ounce package cream cheese
1   cup powdered sugar
1   capful lemon juice
½   cup milk
1   medium package Dream Whip

1   prepared graham cracker crust,
    baked
1   20-ounce can cherry, apple, or
    blueberry pie filling

Beat together all ingredients, except pie crust and fruit filling. Place in baked pie shell. Spoon fruit filling on top of mixture. Chill before serving.

Sweet Wafer

2   cups sifted cake or pastry flour
1   teaspoon baking powder
¼   teaspoon salt
½   cup shortening

1   cup sugar
1   well-beaten egg
1½ teaspoons vanilla extract
2   tablespoons heavy cream

Sift together flour, baking powder, and salt. Cream shortening and sugar together until light and fluffy. Add egg and vanilla. Add flour mixture in thirds alternately with heavy cream.

Beat thoroughly, drop by teaspoon onto a greased baking sheet. Place 3 inches apart, bake at 400° for 10 minutes or until brown. Makes about 4 dozen.

We make these for vanilla pudding. They are good with fudge between them also. I make my banana pudding with them.

Stella, Mother, Cassie, and Rachel at Christmas.

Dolly's Favorite Cheesecake Pudding

Bottom Layer:
  1 cup flour
  ½ cup softened butter

  ½ cup pecans or walnuts

Mix flour, softened butter, and nuts. Press into bottom of 13x9-inch cake pan. Bake at 350° for 15 minutes or until slightly browned. Let cool completely.

Middle Layer:
  8 ounces cream cheese
  1 cup sugar
  1 small container Cool Whip

Top Layers:
  3 cups milk
  2 packages chocolate pudding
  1 large container Cool Whip

Next prepare top layer: mix 3 cups milk and 2 packages of pudding and cook as directed on package. Set aside and cool completely.

For middle layer, in a separate bowl, beat cream cheese and sugar. Blend in small container Cool Whip. Spread over cooled bottom layer (nut mixture) in pan.

Then spread cooled top layer (pudding mixture) over the middle layer. Carefully spread the large Cool Whip all over the top.

Pumpkin Roll

½ cup chopped nuts
3 eggs
½ teaspoon salt.
1 cup sugar
2 teaspoons cinnamon

2 teaspoons baking powder
⅔ cup cooked pumpkin, mashed, fresh or canned, drained
¾ cup flour
Powdered sugar

Grease cookie sheet (with sides) and line with waxed paper. Sprinkle with nuts. Beat together eggs and salt. Add remaining ingredients. Mix well. Pour mix over nuts. Bake 15 minutes at 375°. Roll up in clean dish towel while still hot and let cool. Unroll when towel is cool, about 1 hour. Spread filling on pumpkin roll and roll up again and cover with powdered sugar. Slices best when cold.

Filling:

1 8-ounce cream cheese
3 tablespoons butter

1 cup powdered sugar
1 teaspoon vanilla extract

Beat with mixer until smooth.

Apple Crunch

3 large cooking apples, sliced thin
½ cup sugar
¾ teaspoon cinnamon
½ teaspoon salt

½ cup oats, uncooked
3 tablespoons butter or margarine, melted

Preheat oven to 350°. Place apples in 8x8-inch baking pan. Sprinkle with 2 tablespoons sugar, cinnamon, and salt. Toss gently to mix in small bowl with spoon. Stir together remaining sugar, oats, and butter until mix resembles crumbs, sprinkle evenly over apples. Bake 30 minutes or until apples are tender and top is lightly browned. Serves 6.

Mother's Chocolate Fudge Pudding

1 cup flour	½ cup milk
1 teaspoon baking powder	2 tablespoons melted shortening
1 teaspoon salt	1 teaspoon vanilla extract
⅔ cup white sugar	½ cup chopped pecans
6 tablespoons cocoa	1 cup brown sugar

Sift together flour, baking powder, salt, white sugar, and 2 tablespoons cocoa. Add milk, shortening, and vanilla, mix only until smooth. Add pecans. Put in greased, shallow 1-quart baking dish. Mix brown sugar and remaining 4 tablespoons cocoa. Sprinkle over mixture in baking dish. Pour 1½ cups boiling water over top. (This pudding, when baked, has a chocolate sauce on bottom and cake on top.) Bake at 350° for 40 minutes. Serve warm or cold, with cream or ice cream.

White Gingerbread

2 cups flour	½ teaspoon ginger
½ cup butter or margarine	1 teaspoon baking powder
1 cup white sugar	½ teaspoon cinnamon
½ teaspoon baking soda	1 egg, well beaten
¾ cup buttermilk, thick	¼ teaspoon nutmeg

Mix flour, butter, and sugar together as for pie dough. Take out 1 cup of resulting crumbs and set aside in cool place until remainder of cake is mixed.

Add baking soda to buttermilk and beat thoroughly, then combine all other ingredients (including bulk of "pie dough" crumbs) and mix like cake dough. Sprinkle half of reserved crumbs on bottom of well-greased pan (8x10x1 inches). Pour in cake batter, spread evenly, and then sprinkle remaining crumbs evenly over top and bake in a moderate (350°) oven for 30 to 35 minutes or until toothpick comes out clean.

Orange Chip Cookies

½ cup shortening or margarine
¼ cup white sugar
1 cup flour
½ cup brown sugar
½ teaspoon vanilla

1 egg, well beaten
½ teaspoon baking soda
½ teaspoon salt
1 cup dried orange chips

Mix ingredients, adding orange chips last. Drop by teaspoonful onto greased cookie sheet and bake at 350° for 10 minutes.

Gumdrop Cake

½ cup butter
1 cup sugar
2 eggs, beaten
2¼ cups flour
¼ teaspoon salt
2 teaspoons baking powder

¾ cup raisins
1 pound gumdrops (take out blacks), chopped
1 teaspoon vanilla extract
¾ cup milk

Cream butter while adding sugar and beaten eggs. Sift flour, salt, and baking powder together, then pour over chopped candy and raisins. Add vanilla to milk, and add flour mixture and milk to first mixture, alternately. Bake in large greased loaf pan at 275° to 300° for 1½ hours.

Christmas Sweet Potato Pie

3 cups sweet potatoes, cooked and mashed
½ cup margarine or butter
3 cups sugar
1 teaspoon vanilla extract

Dash of nutmeg
4 eggs, beaten
1 small can evaporated milk
Pastry for 10-inch pie

Mix all ingredients (except pastry) together well. Pour into pastry shell. Bake at 350° for 1 hour and 25 minutes, until inserted knife comes out clean.

Coconut Cake

....

Grease and flour 3 cake pans (8x1½ inches). Preheat oven to 325°.

Prepare 1 box yellow Duncan Hines Butter Recipe cake mix, as directed by instructions on package.

Add to batter:

1	stick butter, melted	1	tablespoon Dream Whip powder
7	tablespoons self-rising flour	¼	cup orange juice

Beat all ingredients together for 5 minutes. Do not underbeat; this batter is thick. Bake at 350° for 20 to 30 minutes. Cool and add icing.

Icing:

1½	cups sugar	⅓	cup water
2½	tablespoons light Karo syrup	1	7-ounce jar marshmallow cream
¼	teaspoon cream of tartar	1	teaspoon vanilla extract
2	egg whites	7	ounces coconut

Place all ingredients (except for marshmallow cream, vanilla, and coconut) in a double boiler and beat with electric mixer for 6 to 8 minutes (do not underbeat). Remove from heat, add marshmallow cream and vanilla. Return to heat and beat one minute. Remove from heat, continuing to beat until it's just slightly cool, about one minute. Spread between each layer and on top and sides of cake. (This cake needs to be on a large platter or deep plate, as some of the icing will overflow.) Sprinkle coconut all over top and sides of cake. Serve warm or cold. Good served with peach slices.

Christmas Persimmon Pudding

. . . .

2	cups persimmon pulp	¼	teaspoon salt
3	eggs, separated	1	teaspoon baking soda
1	tablespoon melted butter	1	teaspoon baking powder
1	cup sugar	1	teaspoon cinnamon
1½	cups flour	2	cups buttermilk

Sieve the persimmons (persimmons need to be really ripe) and set over low heat. Add egg yolks and butter. Beat well. Add sugar and heat again. Sift flour with salt, soda, baking powder, and cinnamon. Add to persimmon mixture alternately with buttermilk. Fold in stiffly beaten egg whites; pour into greased 2-quart casserole and bake 40 to 50 minutes at 350°. Serve with whipped cream. This recipe can be halved for smaller families.

This sign is outside the candy store in Dollywood: "Dolly loves candy and she used to beg her sister Willadeene to make homemade candy every day. Dolly was so persistent that her sister used to say: 'You'll just have to have sweet dreams 'cause I'm not makin' you any candy today.' So 'Sweet Dreams' was a natural name for the candy shop!"

Chocolate Fudge

2 cups sugar
⅓ cup cocoa
½ teaspoon salt

⅔ cup heavy cream
1 teaspoon vanilla
½ stick butter

Mix sugar, cocoa, salt, and cream together. Cook slowly until a drop of the mixture forms a soft ball in a cup of water. Remove from heat and add vanilla and butter. Stir until creamy, then pour into a buttered pan. Mother used to put the candy between saltine crackers while the candy was still soft.

Easy Divinity

2 cups sugar
¼ cup light corn syrup
½ cup water

1 box fluffy frosting mix
1 teaspoon vanilla extract

Combine sugar, corn syrup, water in heavy saucepan. Bring to boil over medium heat, cook to 270°.

Prepare fluffy frosting mix minus 1 tablespoon of the boiling water called for in the package directions. Pour syrup mixture into frosting, beating slowly with mixer. Add vanilla and stir to mix. Drop by teaspoonful onto waxed paper. Allow to cool. May be garnished with pecan halves.

Peanut Brittle

2 cups white sugar
A little baking soda on end of
spoon

1 cup peanuts

Get pan hot. Put sugar in. Stir all the time, stir out lumps. When sugar is all gone to syrup, stir in soda and nuts. Pour on greased pan. Let cool.

Karo Sea Foam

3 cups sugar (2 cups white with 1 cup brown)	½ teaspoon salt
½ cup white Karo syrup	2 egg whites
⅔ cup water	1 teaspoon vanilla
	1 cup chopped nuts

Dissolve sugar, syrup, water, and salt. Cook to hard ball stage. Gradually pour over the 2 egg whites that have been beaten stiff. Beat constantly, add vanilla and nuts, and continue beating until cool. Drop by spoonfuls onto waxed paper and allow to cool.

Hard Candy

Powdered sugar	1 cup water
3¾ cups sugar	1 teaspoon peppermint oil
1½ cups light corn syrup	Food coloring

Sprinkle 18x24-inch strip of aluminum foil with powdered sugar. Mix next 3 ingredients. Stir over medium heat until sugar dissolves, boil (no stirring) to 310°. Remove from heat, add oil and color. Pour onto foil. Cool. Break into pieces. Store in airtight container.

Eggnog

(Without the eggs)

1 quart milk	½ cup sugar
1 3¾-ounce package vanilla instant pudding	1 cup whipping cream
	½ teaspoon vanilla extract

Put 2 cups milk into bowl. Add pudding mix. Beat for 2 minutes. Add sugar, whipping cream, and vanilla. Beat 3 minutes. Add remaining milk, mix, chill, and serve.

8

Open-Hearth Cooking on a Cold Winter's Day

In the mountains of east Tennessee, fall usually gives way to winter earlier than the calendar says it will. So a "cold winter's day" for us often comes right on the heels of those crisp, clear October mornings that we treasure so much.

One of the beautiful things about our home ground is the change of the seasons. The transition of summer into winter through the fall has always been invigorating for me. I know a lot of people talk about winter as being a "dead" time of year, so that autumn for them represents a melancholy precursor to a time when the fields lay fallow, the deciduous trees appear dead, birds fly away, many animals burrow underground to sleep out the season, and the whole natural world seems to impatiently hold its breath as it waits for the first signs that spring is coming.

And for me, that autumn-into-winter progression also represents a special shift into different foods—harvest foods—and different ways of preparing and enjoying special dishes. The cold air becomes redolent with the smells of fresh-baked breads, spice cakes, gingerbread, and dark, warm shortbreads. I think the spices of autumn and winter are special to us—in part—because there is a gestalt of spice smells and cold, crisp air and memories that cannot really be explained but only understood in the deepest levels of our beings.

At the first sign of snow, I usually take out my bean pot and my Dutch oven that my brother Floyd gave me years ago, and fill it with a rich soup or thick stew.

I put the pot on the hook in the fireplace to cook the soup or stew slowly throughout the day. I make Dutch oven bread. I pull ashes to the hearth and put the oven—with its lid on—on the ashes. I cook the bread until it's almost done and then turn it over to brown on the other side. Often, when I call Mother or Papa to ask if they want some of my "winter hearth food," I find that they have spent the day doing the same thing as I have, and so we have shared our food and memories once more—perhaps in the best way possible.

Grandma Rena Owens in her flower garden.

MAIN DISHES

Veal and Pork Casserole

1½	pounds pork steak		1	green pepper, chopped
1½	pounds veal steak		¼	pound mild cheese, put through sieve
	Onion seasoning			
	Celery salt		1	can corn
1	package fine noodles		1	tablespoon butter, melted
1	10½-ounce can chicken soup		⅓	cup cracker crumbs

Cut meat into small pieces. Boil with onion seasoning and celery salt until tender, about 45 minutes. Add noodles, soup, and chopped pepper. Cook until noodles are tender, about 25 minutes. Add cheese. Place in buttered baking dish. Cover with corn, butter, then crumbs. Bake in a 350° oven about 30 minutes.

Pot Likker Dumplings

(This recipe has been traveling around for more than 100 years to all the southern states.)

1	large pot turnip greens boiled with ham hocks		½	teaspoon salt
			¼	teaspoon black pepper
2	tablespoons minced onion		1	egg, lightly beaten
1	to 1½ cups unsifted cornmeal			

You must have one large pot of turnip greens boiled with ham hocks. Start from scratch, with turnip greens fresh out of the patch and smoked ham-bone or hocks. Or use canned chopped turnip greens, simmered an hour with the ham, which should already be boiling tender. Mix 2 tablespoons minced onion (fresh, young ones with part of the green tops are best) into cornmeal. Season with salt and black pepper. Stir in enough boiling pot liquid from the greens to make a stiff dough. When slightly cooled, mix in egg thoroughly. Take this by spoonfuls and shape into small patties about ½ inch thick. Add these patties to pot of greens. Cover and simmer 10 to 15 minutes until done.

Creamed Dried Beef

2	tablespoons flour	½	cup cream
3	tablespoons butter	1	pound dried beef
2½	cups milk		Pepper

Mix flour and butter in saucepan over low heat. Slowly add milk and cream. Stir until quite thick. Simmer dried beef in a small amount of water on slow heat until tender, add drained beef to hot cream sauce. Season with pepper to taste.

Eggs with Dried Beef

½	pound dried beef	2	tablespoons milk or water
2	tablespoons butter, melted	2	tablespoons paprika
4	eggs, lightly beaten		

Cover beef (which has been cut into small pieces) with melted butter, sizzle until crisp. Add eggs, which have been beaten with milk and paprika. As soon as eggs begin to set, stir.

Scrambled Eggs, Beef, and Cheese

1	cup dried beef	¼	teaspoon black pepper
1½	cups tomatoes, cubed	4	eggs, beaten
½	cup grated sharp or mild cheese	3	tablespoons butter or oil
⅛	teaspoon red pepper	¼	teaspoon paprika

Chop dried beef, heat in double boiler until warm. Set aside. Heat tomatoes in saucepan, add cheese, red pepper, black pepper, beaten eggs, and butter or oil until creamy, but not dry. Add dried beef. Serve hot on toast, sprinkle with paprika.

As any country person knows, chickens lay eggs daily for a few months, then they slow down or stop altogether. Most of the time we had eggs, but at times we might not be getting more than two or three eggs a day. Mother always prepared them for the younger children (babies) or she fixed them for Papa along with gravy and biscuits before she sent him out to work the farm or one of the many construction jobs he has had. If someone in the house was sick, they got the eggs in eggnog or soft boiled.

Spaghetti and Cheese with Cabbage

4 tablespoons flour	½ pound cheese
4 tablespoons butter, melted	4 cups shredded cabbage
2 cups milk	2 cups cooked spaghetti
1 teaspoon salt	

Make a sauce of the flour, butter, milk, and salt. Shave up the cheese and add it to the hot sauce. Put the cabbage, spaghetti, and sauce in a buttered baking dish in layers and cover the top with buttered breadcrumbs. Cook for 30 minutes in a 350° oven.

This picture of Clint and Danielle (Bobby's children) with Aunt Granny, as Dolly is called, was taken in 1978.

Some people don't seem to think we get snow in Tennessee, but we get snow in the east Tennessee mountains all the time. This is Grandma Lindy in the 1930s.

Scrambled Eggs

6 eggs	7 stuffed olives, sliced
6 tablespoons cream	2 tablespoons chopped onion
2 tablespoons A-1 sauce	2 tablespoons chopped green pepper
¼ teaspoon salt	3 tablespoons butter or margarine

Beat eggs with fork until well-blended. Add cream, steak sauce, and salt. Brown olives, onion, and green pepper in butter or margarine. Add egg mixture. Cook slowly, stirring constantly, until creamy consistency. Serve at once.

In the mountains, or maybe all over the South, many people will not give you their recipes and some will actually leave out an ingredient or add a substitute rather than give out their original. That totally shocks me even now! My brother Randy and his wife, Deb, are two of the best cooks I know, but they will not give out their recipes. When I started trying to get a simple meat recipe I had had many times at their home, they wouldn't budge. And Deb makes a divinity that we all love, but she absolutely won't part with it either.

They even have a recipe for ribs where she does the first half of the recipe and Randy does the last part— and they don't even know what the other one does. So I put it in the book just as they gave it to me. Deb's is first and Randy's part is second. It's very good, but I think they both left something out, because they knew they would both read my book along with everyone else they know.

Randy and Deb's Pork Ribs

Deb's Part:

Add 1 jar pickling spices (McCormick's is the best) to slowly boiling water. Let steep for about 10 minutes, then add 3 to 5 pounds pork ribs. Parboil ribs in water, just enough to cover them. Cook ribs until almost tender, about 20 minutes. Take ribs out, don't rinse, and give them to your husband to do his special part.

Randy's Part:

Take parboiled ribs, add garlic powder, Cajun spice, lightly sprinkle with salt and pepper. Put on charcoal grill, with onion and pineapple spears. Baste heavily with teriyaki sauce. I've found that the true Polynesian teriyaki sauce is the best even if you have to purchase it from a Polynesian restaurant. Baste and turn ribs approximately every 5 to 7 minutes. You don't want to burn your sauce. Cook about 30 minutes. You can never use too much teriyaki sauce (but don't tell Deb).

Backbones and Ribs

3 to 4 pounds backbones and ribs
1 tablespoon salt

1 medium onion, chopped
1 small red dried whole pepper

Boil ingredients until meat is tender (about 2 hours). Keep enough water added so meat won't stick. Remove pepper before serving.

Backbones and Ribs with Sauerkraut

Use 3 to 4 pounds lean meat (beef or pork); dust with flour. In a large saucepan, brown meat in butter. Add 2 cups tomato juice, 1 large onion (chopped), ½ teaspoon chili powder, 1 teaspoon sugar. Let this cook 1½ to 2 hours or until tender. Add a large can of kraut and let cook 30 minutes longer.

Pork Chops and Gravy

6 pork chops
¼ cup flour
2 teaspoons salt (seasoned salt may
    be used)

Ground black pepper
½ teaspoon powdered mustard
2 tablespoons butter or shortening
2 cups cream or milk

Use lean meat or cut part of fat off. Dust heavily with flour, salt, pepper, and mustard. Brown in skillet with butter. Cover and let simmer 30 minutes. Remove lid, pour milk into skillet. Let it cook slowly about 20 minutes. This makes a brown rich gravy.

Beef and Black-Eyed Peas

....

1	pound ground beef or pork	½	teaspoon salt
¼	cup chopped onion	⅛	teaspoon pepper
1	clove garlic	½	cup tomato ketchup
2¼	cups black-eyed peas, cooked	1	teaspoon all-purpose flour
1	pint tomatoes, cut up	½	cup shredded sharp cheese
1	teaspoon Worcestershire sauce		

In a skillet cook beef, onion, and garlic. Drain. Stir in peas, tomatoes, Worcestershire sauce, salt, and pepper. Bring to a boil. Simmer 15 minutes. Blend ketchup and flour and stir into mixture. Cook and stir until mixture bubbles. Remove from heat and put in a serving dish. Sprinkle with shredded cheese.

Pork or Beef Hash

....

3	cups cooked pork or beef		Celery salt to taste
3	medium potatoes		Garlic seasoning to taste
2	onions, small	½	teaspoon pepper
3	medium carrots	3	tablespoons melted butter
¾	teaspoon salt, more if needed	2	cups soft breadcrumbs
1¼	cups milk		

Grind meat with coarse blade. Dice potatoes, onions, and carrots. Add ingredients except butter and breadcrumbs. Place in well-greased pan, cover top with buttered breadcrumbs. Place in 350° oven and bake about 1½ hours. Half a can of tomato soup may be baked with meat.

Barbecued Ribs

. . . .

1	cup ketchup	1	teaspoon celery salt
2	cups water	3	to 4 pounds beef or pork ribs
¼	cup brown sugar	4	tablespoons chopped onion
¼	cup cider vinegar		Salt and pepper
¼	cup Worcestershire sauce		Lemon juice
1	teaspoon chili powder		

Combine first 7 ingredients in a saucepan and bring to a full boil. Cool and store in refrigerator.

Spread ribs in a large low pan. Sprinkle with chopped onion, salt, pepper, and lemon juice. Bake at 300° for 45 minutes. Drain off fat and cover with some of above sauce. Bake another 25 minutes.

In 1971 my mother planned a special time with all her daughters. It was then that she gave us back all the true romance magazines she had taken from us for not washing dishes or doing other chores. One evening Stella, Dolly, myself, and Cassie had a slumber party and read the magazines.

Sausage Stack Supreme

1½ pounds bulk pork sausage
1 cup packaged herb seasoned stuffing
2 tablespoons butter
1 cup finely chopped tart apples
½ cup finely chopped celery

¼ cup minced onion
2 tablespoons snipped parsley
2 tablespoons chili sauce
¼ teaspoon dry mustard
¼ teaspoon pepper

Preheat oven to 375°. Shape sausage into 12 thin patties, ¼ inch thick. Prepare 1 cup stuffing according to package directions, using ¼ cup water and 2 tablespoons butter or margarine. Add tart apples, celery, onion, and seasoning; toss to mix. Arrange 6 sausage patties in an 8x12-inch shallow pan. Top each with ½ cup stuffing then another patty; toothpick through center to hold. Bake 45 minutes or until done. (Remember, to double the recipe, one must double each ingredient.)

Liver in Baked Onions

½ pound calf's liver
10 slices bacon
1 cup chopped celery, soaked in ice water
½ teaspoon salt
Celery salt

Paprika
Onion seasoning
6 or 8 medium onions
¼ cup butter, melted
Breadcrumbs

Scald liver in boiling water about 2 minutes. Remove skin and put through food chopper. Cut bacon in small pieces and fry until crisp. Add liver, celery, and seasoning to bacon. Remove outer skin of onions, remove center and leave firm shell. Fill with liver, bacon mixture, sprinkle top with buttered breadcrumbs and bake in 300° oven using baking pan with a little water. Bake about 1 hour.

VEGETABLES AND SIDE DISHES

Creamed Cabbage

. . . .

1	small head cabbage	Small amount cider vinegar
⅛	teaspoon pepper	1 egg
⅛	teaspoon salt	1 cup cream
1	tablespoon butter, melted	

Cut cabbage, cook until tender, in just enough water so cabbage will be almost dry when done. Season with pepper, salt, butter, and a little vinegar. Beat egg, add cream. Stir in quickly before removing from heat. Do not let mixture boil after adding cream as it will curdle.

Milk Mush

. . . .

7½	tablespoons cornmeal	1 cup boiling water
2	tablespoons flour	Salt to taste
1	cup light cream	

Moisten meal and flour with a little cream, stir into boiling salted water. When smooth, cook 5 minutes. Add a little cream or butter. Serve hot.

Cornmeal Gravy

. . . .

Fry about 4 or 5 pieces of side meat or bacon. Have enough shortening in pan to cover ½ cup cornmeal. Add about ½ cup of meal and 1 teaspoon of salt. Brown meal to a light brown. Then add 2½ cups of milk. Stir until it boils. Serve while hot.

Dolly sure does enjoy performing. (Courtesy of Deborah Poole)

Baked Rutabagas or Turnips

. . . .

2 cups rutabagas, cooked and mashed	1 teaspoon salt
¼ teaspoon mace	⅛ teaspoon ground ginger
2 tablespoons butter	1 egg, beaten
1 cup breadcrumbs	1 tablespoon sugar
¼ teaspoon pepper	½ cup milk
	2 tablespoons butter, melted

Preheat the oven to 350°. Combine rutabagas with all ingredients except melted butter. Turn the mixture into a buttered 1-quart casserole dish. Brush the top with the melted butter. Bake about 45 minutes, until brown.

BREADS AND CEREALS

Bacon Biscuits

· ·

2 cups flour
1 tablespoon baking powder
3 to 4 tablespoons bacon fat

½ cup milk
8 to 10 slices of bacon, cooked and
   crumbled, fat reserved

Sift flour and baking powder together, mix in bacon fat. Add milk to make a soft dough. Fold in bacon, roll out on a floured surface, cut out, and bake at 400° about 15 minutes or until brown.

My pretty cousin Rena Conley (Aunt Dorothy Jo's daughter) is the one that introduced me to Rutledge Hill Press. She is responsible for the publication of my last two books. Thank you, Rena!

Batch breads—a batch of bread or batter bread—was what one made in a hurry. There was absolutely no style to this pan of bread and Papa was well known for making it when he had to cook a meal or help out around the house.

It was just flour, salt, baking powder, shortening, and milk or water, stirred together—no measurements—and poured into a large pan and baked. It tasted good to us. My mother rarely measured what she cooked. How could you measure a gallon of beans or 6 cups of flour when you only had a half gallon of beans and 4 cups of flour? She cooked what she had and added "extenders" to a lot of things. Of course, her stone soup, salmon stew, chocolate gravy, and tomato gravy are just a few of the many meals she fixed that are still some of our favorite foods—along with cowboy beans, fried potatoes, and dryland fish.

Indian Bean Bread

4 cups cornmeal
2 cups mashed cooked pinto beans
½ teaspoon baking soda
2 cups boiling water

Put cornmeal into bowl, mix in beans that have been drained. Hollow out in meal a place to put soda and water. Make a dough stiff enough to form balls the size of a large egg. Drop balls into a pot of boiling water. Cook about 4 or 5 minutes or until done. Serve with cooked greens and pork.

Cornmeal Flapjacks

1 cup buttermilk
1 cup water
½ cup flour
1 teaspoon baking soda
1 teaspoon salt
2 cups cornmeal, sifted

Mix first five ingredients. Stir in sifted cornmeal and mix until thick. Then drop spoonfuls into hot grease, like pancakes. Brown on each side. Serve while hot with butter or use for bread with any food. Add an egg if you like.

Cornmeal Pancakes

2 teaspoons sugar	¾ cup cornmeal
1 teaspoon salt	2 eggs, well beaten
1 tablespoon baking powder	1¼ cups milk
1¼ cups sifted flour	3 tablespoons melted shortening

Sift together sugar, salt, baking powder, and flour. Stir in cornmeal. Combine eggs and milk and add to mixture. Add shortening and mix until smooth. Drop by tablespoonfuls onto lightly greased hot griddle. Cook until edges are brown and bubbles are in middle. Turn and cook on other side. Serve butter and sorghum with pancakes.

Chocolate Gravy

1 cup sugar	⅓ stick butter
2 tablespoons cocoa	1 teaspoon vanilla
4 tablespoons flour	
4 cups milk or 3 cups if you want thicker gravy	

Pour sugar, cocoa, and flour in skillet. Turn on heat, then add milk gradually. Cook until thick. Add butter and vanilla while it's cooling. Serve with biscuits.

Uncle Bill and Uncle Alden used to get in the kitchen with us and we'd cook up bread and soup while the women folk—Grandma Rena Owens, Aunt Estelle, Aunt Dorothy Jo—visited Mother. Uncle Louis and Uncle Henry would do what most older children do and pick on the younger ones. They would always go through the kitchen a couple of times telling us we were going to be in trouble for cooking and messing up the kitchen, but we never were.

Cornmeal Gruel 1

1½ cups meat or vegetable stock   ⅓ teaspoon salt
    (water can be used if you do not   1 slightly rounded tablespoon
    have stocks; use 3 beef bouillon   cornmeal
    cubes)

Have stock or water salted and actively boiling, shake the meal gently into it, and cook 20 minutes, stirring constantly. Then turn the mixture into a double boiler and cook 2 hours. The gruel will be a liquid. Strain if desired.

Cornmeal Gruel 2

5 tablespoons cornmeal   1 quart boiling water
¼ teaspoon salt   1 cup milk, heated
1 teaspoon sugar

Mix cornmeal, salt, and sugar into thin paste with a little cold water. Add quart of boiling water, cook 3 hours. Add milk or cream.

Corn Bread Sticks

½ cup margarine or butter, melted   1 egg, beaten
1 cup self-rising cornmeal   1 cup buttermilk
½ cup flour

Grease cast-iron corn stick pan with small amount of margarine. Mix together melted margarine, cornmeal, flour, egg, and buttermilk. Pour ingredients into heated corn stick pan and bake at 350° for 30 minutes.

Fritters or Corn Griddle Cakes

....

1½ cups sifted flour	6 tablespoons condensed milk or
2 teaspoons baking powder	half-and-half
¾ teaspoon salt	2¼ cups drained whole kernel corn,
2 tablespoons sugar	canned or fresh
3 tablespoons shortening	Oil, for frying
2 eggs, well beaten	

Sift together flour, baking powder, salt, and sugar. Work in shortening. Mix eggs and milk. Add egg mixture to flour all at once, mixing quickly but thoroughly. Fold in corn. Drop by teaspoon into 2 inches of fat, hot enough to brown an inch bread cube in about 55 seconds (360°). Fry a few at a time until brown, drain on paper towel. Serves 6.

For corn griddle cakes add ¼ cup or 2 tablespoons of cornmeal. Cook in ⅛ inch hot shortening, until edges are cooked. Then turn and brown other side. Makes 12 cakes about 4½ inches across.

These are good with tomato soup, ham slices, green onions and cooked greens (turnip or spinach), lemon pudding or custard for dessert.

Fried Cornmeal Mush

....

Slowly add 1 cup yellow cornmeal to 4 cups boiling salted water. Stir, cook until thick, then cook 3 hours in double boiler. Use as a cereal, or pack cooked cornmeal in greased loaf pan to cool. Cut in slices, fry slowly until brown. Serve with butter and syrup.

DESSERTS AND SWEETS

Shortnin' Bread

. . . .

½ pound butter or margarine
  (2 sticks)
6 rounded tablespoons powdered
  sugar

2 cups sifted flour
1 cup chopped nuts
1 teaspoon vanilla extract
  Additional powdered sugar

Preheat oven to 300°. Mix butter and sugar together. Add flour, nuts, and vanilla. Roll small pieces of dough between palms of hands into balls. Bake on lightly floured baking sheet about 15 to 20 minutes. Fill paper bag with powdered sugar. When cakes are cool, shake carefully in bag until coated with sugar. Place in bowl as cakes are coated. Pour remaining sugar over them. Cover until ready to serve.

Dale Puckett (left) *and Dolly are first cousins. They are shown a few years earlier on page 65.*

Cake Crumb Pudding

3 eggs, lightly beaten
⅓ cup butter, melted
4 teaspoons jelly
1 cup rich milk (light cream)

1 cup sugar
2 cups dry cake crumbs
1 teaspoon vanilla extract

Combine all ingredients, bake at 300° for 45 minutes in a well-buttered baking dish, which is sitting in pan with a little hot water (water bath). Serve with hard sauce or pudding sauce.

Bread Pudding

2 cups stale breadcrumbs
1 pint cream or milk
½ cup sugar
4 tablespoons butter, melted

4 eggs
Few grains salt
½ teaspoon vanilla
¼ teaspoon cinnamon

Soak breadcrumbs in cream. Add sugar and butter, beaten eggs, salt, and flavoring. Place in buttered baking dish. Sprinkle with cinnamon. Bake in 275° oven about 35 minutes, placing dish in hot water while baking. Serve with a pinch of grated orange peel, chopped raisins and dates, and cream.

Candied Popcorn

3 quarts popped corn—no salt
1 cup sugar

1 tablespoon butter or margarine
3 tablespoons water

Mix sugar, butter, and water in a saucepan.
Bring to boil. Cook to 220°. Pour immediately over popped corn and stir until dry. You can add a drop of food coloring to syrup just before stirring into popcorn. Several colors mixed together look great.

Brown Sugar Fudge

1½   cups white sugar
1¼   cups brown sugar
¼   teaspoon salt
1   12-ounce can evaporated milk

2   tablespoons light Karo syrup
1   teaspoon vanilla extract
¼   cup (½ stick) butter
½   to 1 cup chopped nuts (optional)

Mix sugars, salt, milk and Karo syrup together. Cook until mixture forms a soft ball when dropped into a cup of cold water. Remove from heat. Add vanilla and butter. Stir until creamy. Add nuts if you like. Stir mixture and pour into buttered pan.

Taffy Tips

THE higher the temperature to which a taffy is cooked, the harder it is. The addition of butter or fat makes it less likely to stick to the teeth.

Pulling taffy: Handle the cooled mass; knead into a mass suitable for pulling, adding flavoring and coloring. If taffy is sticky, dust hands with powdered sugar and work slowly until cool enough to handle easily. Taffy that becomes too hard to pull may be held over heat to soften. Several changes occur during the pulling: it becomes lighter in color, more elastic, and very glossy with tiny bubbles or air pockets all through it.

Cutting Taffy: Pull into cylinders of desired thickness, roll under the palms of hands until smooth, and cut into suitable lengths with scissors (buttering blades prevents sticking). Wrapping each piece in waxed paper makes taffy last longer and keeps it from getting sticky.

Honey Taffy

1   cup strained honey
    Few grains salt

1   cup sugar
1   tablespoon butter

Boil honey, salt, and sugar to hard ball stage, 265° to 270°. Add butter. Pour into well-buttered pan. Cool. Pull until white and porous. Cut into 1-inch pieces.

Molasses Taffy

· · · · · · · · · · · · · · · · · · · ·

1½ cups molasses	½ cup water
1½ cups sugar	¼ teaspoon salt
1½ teaspoons cider vinegar	3 tablespoons butter

Combine molasses, sugar, vinegar, water, and salt in heavy saucepan. Place over low heat and stir constantly until sugar is dissolved. Boil moderately to 240° (soft ball).

Add the butter. Boil slowly to 265° to 270° (hard ball). Stir frequently during the last part of cooking.

Remove from heat. Wipe pouring surface of the pan and pour at once onto an oiled surface.

Cool until comfortable to handle. Pull and cut into pieces. Makes about 1 pound.

Saltwater Taffy

· · · · · · · · · · · · · · · · · · · ·

2 cups sugar	2 teaspoons glycerin
1 cup light corn syrup	2 tablespoons butter
1½ cups water	Flavoring and food color if
1½ teaspoons salt	desired

Combine sugar, syrup, water, salt, and glycerin in heavy saucepan. Place over low heat and stir until sugar is dissolved. Then cook without stirring to hard ball (260° to 300°).

Remove from heat, add butter, and pour the taffy onto an oiled surface of a shallow pan, marble slab, or platter. Cool until comfortable to handle; flavor and color; gather into ball. Pull and cut. Makes about 1¼ pounds.

Taffy may be divided into 3 or 4 parts and each part flavored differently, lemon, lime, vanilla, etc. Color with food coloring to correspond. We just used vanilla, probably 1 teaspoon, and left the taffy the natural color.

9

Mother's Recipes —Our Favorites

Well, I've saved the best for last, I guess. I don't know whether these dishes are our favorites because Mother made them so "good," or whether Mother made them so good because they were our favorites. We always liked chicken and eggs, so it doesn't really matter which came first.

Anyway, "they" (whoever "they" may be) often say that food memories, especially those associated with the best food smells coming out of the kitchen, are some of the strongest memories that we have. When I read these recipes over, I can still smell those stuffed peppers, with the steam rising up out of them and the sweet smell of the peppers and onions mixing with the pungent aroma of spices and meats. Or the smell of Mother's chili, with its wonderful blend of spices, beans, meat, and tomatoes. She used coffee in the ingredients and I have never found anyone else that does. Talk about using leftovers! Mother also made a sweet spice cake that some of the children called a "naked cake" because it had no icing.

I've noticed that our favorites seem to be those that are savory and perhaps best appreciated in the fall and winter months. I remember how special it was to come into Mother's warm kitchen on a cold day and smell those wonderful aromas. I think our sense of smell must be heightened by that transition, when we come in from the cold and meet those warm, comforting smells that we learned to associate with the special caring and loving that Mother put into her preparation of those dishes.

I can remember our sense of anticipation as we savored the smells coming from Mother's kitchen, and I certainly remember our sense of comfort and satisfaction as we savored the dishes themselves. Food and memory. Maybe that's just as important in our family as music and memory.

Perhaps someday they'll invent a way to make cookbooks that come with the wonderful smells of the recipes in the books. Until then, go ahead, cook up a pot of Mother's bean vegetable soup and see if it makes a memory for you and your family, too. I hope it does. And the meatloaf and the stuffed peppers and the stone soup (see page vi for recipe), and all the other dishes that were "our favorites"— well, just maybe some of them will become yours, too. I hope so.

Stuffed Peppers 1

4 green bell peppers	1½ cups precooked rice
½ pound ground beef	½ teaspoon salt
¼ pound ground pork	¼ teaspoon pepper
⅔ cup ketchup	¼ cup grated cheese

Cut tops from peppers and remove seeds. Parboil until tender. Brown beef and pork, add tomato ketchup, rice, and seasoning. Stuff peppers with mixture and garnish with grated cheese. Place peppers in baking dish and bake at 350° for 30 minutes.

Stuffed Peppers 2

6 large green bell peppers	1 teaspoon salt
5 cups boiling water, salted	⅛ teaspoon garlic salt
1 pound hamburger meat	1 cup cooked rice
2 tablespoons chopped onions	1 15-ounce can tomato sauce

Slice tops off peppers. Remove membrane and seeds. Cook in boiling salt water for 5 minutes. Drain. Sauté hamburger and onion in skillet. Drain off fat. Stir in salt, garlic salt, rice, and tomato sauce. Heat thoroughly. Remove from heat and stuff peppers with sauce. Place in baking dish. Pour remaining sauce over peppers. Bake approximately 20 minutes at 350°.

We didn't always have milk in our house since we only had one milk cow. So several weeks or at least a couple of months a year, we bought milk from our neighbors along with butter and buttermilk. Milk, with the cream still on it, was 35 cents a gallon, I think. We also used canned milk. There was also a brand of powdered or dry milk we bought at those times. I remember Grandma Rena Owens used it a lot.

Stuffed Peppers 3

1 pound hamburger
½ cup uncooked rice
1 small chopped onion

Salt
Pepper
6 large green bell peppers

Combine rice, onion, and seasonings. Cover with water and simmer until boiled down and rice is done. Fill green peppers with mixture and bake at 350° until peppers are done (about 1 hour). Add a little water to bottom of pan while peppers are baking. This is a recipe I sort of just throw together as it's been in my family for years and at the time it originated, they never really measured anything, so it can be adjusted to suit taste.

Mother's Salmon Stew

1 12-ounce can whole kernel corn
1 17-ounce can sweet peas
1 15½-ounce can pink salmon, crushed, most of skin and bones removed

6 medium onions, chopped
1 stick butter
1 quart water
1 46-ounce can tomato juice

Mix all ingredients except tomato juice. Do not drain the liquid from any of the cans. Bring to a boil, boil for 20 minutes, then simmer for 15 minutes. Add tomato juice and simmer for 5 minutes.

Add:

1 quart milk
1 small can evaporated milk
Dash salt

Dash cayenne pepper
2 teaspoons salt
1 teaspoon pepper

Simmer for a few minutes and serve with crackers. Makes about 2 gallons.

Black-Eyed Peas

3   strips of bacon
1   can green beans
2   cans black-eyed peas
1   can beef bouillon
1   teaspoon beef bouillon granules
¼   teaspoon cayenne pepper
½   teaspoon black pepper

½   teaspoon salt
½   teaspoon parsley flakes or 1
    teaspoon fresh parsley
½   teaspoon garlic powder
2   potatoes, peeled and sliced ½ inch
    thick

Fry bacon in large pan until well-done, drain grease from pan, and set bacon aside. Pour beans, black-eyed peas, and bouillon into pan. (This can also be transferred into a large pot to cook.) Stir in bouillon granules and seasonings. Place potatoes on top. Cook until potatoes are tender. When done, sprinkle bacon on top and serve.

Mother's Chili

½   gallon white navy beans, cooked,
    undrained
1   pound ground beef or pork, fried,
    but not brown
1   large bottle ketchup (we use 1
    pint)
2   medium onions, chopped

2   cups strong coffee
    Salt and pepper to taste
    Dash cayenne
    Enough chili powder to make it
    hot as you like it (we use 1
    teaspoon)

Combine and simmer these ingredients for 45 minutes to 1 hour. Serves 10 to 12. Very good with hot dogs.

Mother used to shell corn in early November and then parch a panful to snack on. Put some bacon grease or cooking oil in a shallow baking pan with salt. Add corn. Bake at 300°, stirring often, until deep brown. A crunchy snack.

Depression Coffee

2 cups corn, parched really brown, cracked

1 cup molasses

Spread parched corn in pan, then pour molasses over corn. Put into the oven at 225°. Cook until dry, stirring often. When cool, store in coffee tin.

To make coffee, add 2 teaspoons of mixture per cup of boiling water, then simmer 3 or 4 minutes. Strain and serve with cream if desired.

Old-fashioned Home Baked Beans

1 pound white beans
¼ cup brown sugar
1 teaspoon salt
1 teaspoon dry mustard

¼ cup molasses
3 or 4 cups water
½ pound salt pork
2 or 3 onions, chopped fine

Soak beans overnight. Drain, wash, and parboil 15 to 20 minutes until tender. Mix dry ingredients and molasses in measuring cup. Fill with water, mix. Pour over beans in bean pot. Cover the beans with water. Scald and scrape the salt pork, cut into bite-size pieces. Stir the pork and onions in the beans. Cover and bake at 250° for 7 or 8 hours. Add water every 2 hours or as needed. Remove cover for last 2 hours to brown beans. I use 4 strips of fried bacon with most of the fat drained off instead of salt pork.

Mother and Papa at home in 1972.

Sloppy Joes

1	medium onion, chopped	½	teaspoon pepper	
2	tablespoons butter	2	tablespoons lemon juice	
2	pounds hamburger	2	tablespoons brown sugar	
½	cup celery, chopped	2	tablespoons Worcestershire sauce	
1	teaspoon dry mustard	1	cup water	
2	teaspoons salt	1	tablespoon vinegar	

Fry onions in butter, add hamburger, and brown. Mix remaining ingredients in bowl and add to hamburger. Simmer 20 minutes. Serve on buns.

Cousin Debbie Jo (Aunt Dorothy Jo's pretty daughter) makes us all sound good when she sings background on the road and in the studio. She has worked the road with Dolly, Randy, Freida, Floyd, and Rachel. She also worked at Dollywood for several years.

Bean Vegetable Soup

1	cup fresh string beans, sliced	1	cup fresh spinach, chopped
1½	cups fresh green lima beans	3	tablespoons butter
2	carrots, thinly sliced	1	tablespoon flour
1	cup cauliflower, diced	2	quarts hot milk
3	small new potatoes, peeled and quartered	⅜	cup light fresh cream
4	radishes, cut in half	1	cup cooked, cleaned shrimp, coarsely chopped
1	tablespoon salt	2	tablespoons fresh parsley, finely chopped
1	tablespoon sugar		

Place string beans, lima beans, carrots, cauliflower, potatoes, and radishes in a large kettle, cover with water, add salt and sugar. Cover and cook gently until tender, about 40 minutes. Add spinach and cook 10 minutes longer. Melt butter in large soup kettle and blend in flour until smooth. Stir in hot milk until smooth. Add cream and stir into milk gently. Add vegetables with liquid and shrimp, heat thoroughly. Soup should be thick. Serve in hot soup bowls and garnish with parsley. Serves 8 people.

Mother's Salmon Patties

(From Stella's cookbook *Country Cooking*)

2	eggs, beaten	4	tablespoons flour
1	small chopped onion	1	15-ounce can salmon (do not
	Salt and pepper		drain)

In a large mixing bowl, mix all ingredients into a stiff batter. Drop batter by heaping tablespoons into hot oil and fry until brown on both sides.

Cornmeal Liver Mush

2	cups liver	1	to 1½ cups chicken stock
¾	cup fat	1	teaspoon sage
¾	cup cornmeal		Salt and pepper

Cook liver in fat until well-done. Grind liver and fat. Parch cornmeal good and brown. Add stock and stir until good and thick. Then add liver and fat. Add sage. Salt and pepper to taste. This is also good with potatoes cubed fine and cooked and ½ cup onions cut fine, sautéd until clear. This is what we called liver hash.

Mother's Baked Pork Chops

1	large onion, thinly sliced		Pepper
1	orange, peeled, thinly sliced	4	to 6 pork chops (preferably center
	Salt		cut)

In a shallow baking dish, place a layer of onions and oranges; salt and pepper pork chops on both sides and place in dish. Top with layer of onions and oranges. Bake, covered, at 350° for 2 hours. Brown under broiler if necessary.

Souse Meat

Because we grew up on this kind of food and still think it a tasty treat, I have substituted a cut of meat you can get at the grocery store. I usually make it after Thanksgiving and Christmas from leftover turkey and ham.

3   pounds of turkey or ham (I mix   ½   teaspoon sage
    my leftovers from holidays.)   Salt and pepper to taste
½   cup cider vinegar
1   small red pepper (dried pod,
    crumbled)

Put leftover turkey or ham into a large pot with 3 cups of water, cook until meat is loose from bone, about 30 minutes. Remove, take off the bone. Set aside broth. Chop and pull meat into small pieces. Return meat to broth and add rest of ingredients. Set aside and cool to room temperature. Most of the liquid should be cooked out of the meat now. Pour into a large loaf pan, cover. Let set in refrigerator until firm. Use as a lunch meat, sliced for sandwiches or on crackers. Can be served with corn bread and a salad as a meal.

This picture of an Odd Fellows picnic on Tazewell Pike, near Knoxville, was taken about 1920. (Courtesy of Knox County Two Centuries Photograph Project, McClung Historical Collection, Knox County Public Library System)

Mother is a good cook, but when I was trying to get recipes from her, I realized she has no clear idea how she does it. She makes macaroni and tomatoes, backbones and ribs with whole pods of hot red peppers that stay warm on the tip of the tongue and lips, long after we leave the table.

She used to dry pumpkin and apples. We called the apples dried fruit, and it was used for stack cakes and fried pies. We still make dried green beans that are known by several names. We call them "shab beans" or "shuck beans." Some of our relatives call them "leather britches."

Scrapple

Scrapple is a nourishing meal. Take the heart, tongue (that has been properly skinned and cleaned), kidneys, and any lean scraps of pork, and boil it until it will slip easily from the bones. Remove the fat, gristle, and bones; then chop fine. Set aside the liquid in which the meat was boiled until cold. Take the cake of fat from the surface, and return the pot to the fire. When it boils, put in the chopped meat, and season well with pepper and salt. Let it boil again. Then thicken with cornmeal as you would in making cornmeal mush. Cook 1 hour, stirring constantly at first, then putting back on the stove to boil gently. When done, pour in a long mold. This can be kept several weeks in cold weather. Cut in slices and fry brown as you do mush.

Liver Loaf

Liver, cooked, chopped or mashed
Eggs, hard-boiled, chopped or mashed
Mayonnaise (or tomato ketchup)

Onions, chopped very fine
Salt
Pepper

Season to taste and mix to consistency you prefer.

Cornmeal Gravy with Liver

· · · · · · · · · · · · · · · · · · ·

4   slices of liver
    Salt, pepper to taste
¾   cup cornmeal

Oil for frying
½   cup milk
1   cup water

Season liver with salt and pepper and roll in cornmeal. Fry in plenty of grease or oil, having enough cornmeal left to make the gravy. Add the remaining cornmeal to hot grease, letting it brown well. Then add milk, water, salt, and pepper. Cook until done. Serve with liver or any kind of fresh meats.

We made cottage cheese from milk. Mother would put a couple of gallons of milk on the stove that was just warm. It took several hours to make, but it was worth it. When the cheese separated from the whey, she lifted it from the whey. She did a quick rinse, added a cup of cream off the fresh milk, stored it in the spring house—later the refrigerator when we got one—until dinner or supper, as we called it.

Baked Hominy

· · · · · · · · · · · · · · · · · · ·

    Large can of hominy (#2½; whole
    hominy, white or yellow)
1   large onion, chopped
1   small red or green pepper (or
    mixed), chopped

1   cup grated Cheddar cheese
1   8-ounce can tomato sauce
½   teaspoon chili powder
½   teaspoon black pepper
½   cup breadcrumbs (corn bread)

Mix all ingredients. Put in baking dish and bake 45 minutes at 350°.

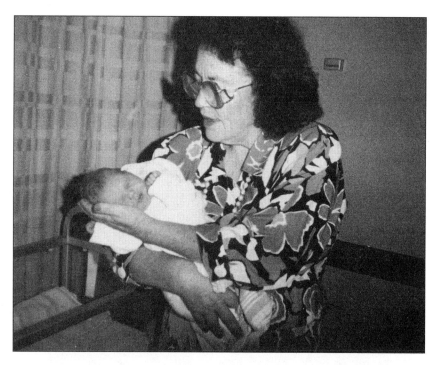

Mother, shown here with her great-niece Cassie Styles, could always hush a crying baby.

Mother's Meatloaf

. . . .

2	to 3 pounds hamburger (extra lean for less fat)	1	15- to 16-ounce can whole kernel corn, drained
¼	to ½ teaspoon paprika	1	onion, chopped fine
1	teaspoon onion salt	1	egg
1	to 2 teaspoons garlic powder	½	stack of Ritz crackers, crumbled
1	tablespoon parsley	⅓	cup milk
	Salt and pepper	1	15- to 16-ounce can sweet peas, drained
1	tablespoon steak sauce		
1	bell pepper, chopped		

Preheat oven to 350°. Combine all ingredients except egg, crackers, milk, and peas. In separate bowl, mix egg, crackers, and milk. Add egg mixture to meat and mix well. Add peas last and stir to blend. Bake in 9x9-inch pan for 1 hour.

Grandma's Meatloaf

2 pounds ground beef	1 cup tomato soup
½ pound ground pork	2 teaspoons salt
1 medium onion, chopped	½ teaspoon pepper
2 eggs, beaten	1 small can peas (optional)
1 cup oatmeal	

Mix well and pack firmly in 9x9-inch pan. Bake 1½ hours at 350°. Cut in squares.

Grandma Lindy Owen (left) was the mother of Aunt Estelle *(in door-way),* my mother *(not in picture),* and Aunt Dorothy Jo *(right).*

Meatloaf with Corn Bread Topping

1½ pounds ground chuck
1   pound extra lean pork breakfast
    sausage (the pork and turkey mix
    is very good)
1½ cups cooked rice

1   egg, beaten
1   teaspoon salt
½   teaspoon pepper
½   teaspoon parsley
1   small onion, chopped

Preheat oven to 350°. Mix ingredients together and lightly press into two small pans or one large pan. (A double loaf pan that drains the grease is preferable.) The top of the loaves should be flat to make an even surface for the topping. Spread topping evenly on top of the meatloaf and bake about 60 minutes. Serve hot.

Corn Bread Topping:

1   cup flour
1   teaspoon baking powder
½   teaspoon salt
¼   teaspoon sage
2   tablespoons shortening
¾   cup milk

½   cup cornmeal
2   teaspoons sugar
⅛   teaspoon pepper
¼   teaspoon thyme
2   eggs, beaten

Mix well. Add more milk if needed. Pour over meatloaf.

Fried Tomatoes

Slice green tomatoes and season with salt and pepper. Dip the slices into beaten egg mixture. Roll the slices in flour and fry in oil or bacon grease until browned.

Cowboy Beans

· · · · · · · · · · · · · · · · · · · ·

1	pound ground beef	1	teaspoon cider vinegar
2	medium onions, chopped fine	3	tablespoons brown sugar
1	small bell pepper, chopped fine	2	teaspoons mustard
1	28-ounce can pork and beans, or	1	teaspoon salt
	1 quart cooked October beans	1	teaspoon pepper
2	cups ketchup		

Brown ground beef, onions, and pepper. Add remaining ingredients. Pour into baking dish and bake at 300° for about 25 minutes.

Baked Onions

· · · · · · · · · · · · · · · · · · · ·

12	medium onions, peeled and whole	4	teaspoons brown sugar (can use white)
4	tablespoons butter		

Cook onions in boiling water in saucepan until tender, about 20 minutes. Pour off extra water, add butter, let melt. Add sugar and bake until brown.

Succotash

· · · · · · · · · · · · · · · · · · · ·

Mix 2 cups cooked lima beans and 2 cups cooked corn, cut from cob. (Chopped green, red, or yellow bell peppers may be added for color and flavor.) Season with salt and pepper, add ½ stick butter and ½ cup milk or cream when thoroughly heated. Serve.

Mother and Papa at home in 1996.

Fried Apples

6   to 8 cooking apples   Sugar
½   stick margarine (or 1 tablespoon
    butter or bacon grease)

Wash, peel, core, and slice apples.

Melt margarine, butter, or bacon grease in a large skillet. Heat to medium hot, put in apples, cover. Turn heat to high until they begin to fry. Turn down to low. Cook slowly approximately 15 minutes or until they are well-cooked. Stir them well and add sugar to taste. Let them simmer 2 or 3 minutes longer.

Index

INDEX

INDEX